Mastering Django

Mastering Django helps the reader master the powerful Django framework for Python for creating dynamic applications and projects.

Django is a high-level, open-source Python web framework created to help web developers achieve tight deadlines while also meeting a variety of needs. The primary feature of Django that makes it so popular among developers is that it promotes rapid development while providing a consistent and realistic design.

Django is a complete toolkit with a basic code and highly adaptable architecture that promotes rapid development – it can shape and pace your web app concept and see it through to launch in a matter of hours.

Django's simplicity, stability, scalability, and flexibility are unmatched. It is currently a vibrant, collaborative, open-source project with thousands of users and contributors. Django is a versatile framework capable of developing any website.

Hallmarks of this popular web framework include Robust design, rapid software development, fantastic documentation and tutorials, a vast community with readymade solutions, reasonably easy learning curve, and a high degree of clarity and readability.

Django has carved out a niche for itself in the industry over the years, and appropriately so. Many popular apps use Django as their secret ingredient. Django has many features and can accommodate any modern web application. If you wish to build a successful career in web development, learning Django is a wise choice.

With *Mastering Django*, learning the Django framework becomes a charm, and will help readers undoubtedly advance their careers.

The *Mastering Computer Science* series is edited by Sufyan bin Uzayr, a writer and educator with more than a decade of experience in the computing field.

Mastering Computer Science
Series Editor: Sufyan bin Uzayr

Mastering Django: A Beginner's Guide
Jaskiran Kaur, NT Ozman, and Reza Nafim

Mastering Ubuntu: A Beginner's Guide
Jaskiran Kaur, Rubina Salafey, and Shahryar Raz

Mastering GNOME: A Beginner's Guide
Jaskiran Kaur, Mathew Rooney, and Reza Nafim

Mastering Flutter: A Beginner's Guide
Divya Sachdeva, NT Ozman, and Reza Nafim

Mastering Rust: A Beginner's Guide
Divya Sachdeva, Faruq KC, and Aruqqa Khateib

Mastering Visual Studio Code: A Beginner's Guide
Jaskiran Kaur, D Nikitenko, and Mathew Rooney

For more information about this series, please visit: https://www.routledge.com/Mastering-Computer-Science/book-series/MCS

The "Mastering Computer Science" series of books are authored by the Zeba Academy team members, led by Sufyan bin Uzayr.

Zeba Academy is an EdTech venture that develops courses and content for learners primarily in STEM fields, and offers education consulting to Universities and Institutions worldwide. For more info, please visit https://zeba.academy

Mastering Django

A Beginner's Guide

Edited by Sufyan bin Uzayr

CRC Press
Taylor & Francis Group
Boca Raton London New York

CRC Press is an imprint of the
Taylor & Francis Group, an **informa** business

First Edition published 2023
by CRC Press
6000 Broken Sound Parkway NW, Suite 300, Boca Raton, FL 33487-2742

and by CRC Press
2 Park Square, Milton Park, Abingdon, Oxon, OX14 4RN

CRC Press is an imprint of Taylor & Francis Group, LLC

© 2023 Sufyan bin Uzayr

Library of Congress Cataloging-in-Publication Data

Names: Bin Uzayr, Sufyan, editor.
Title: Mastering Django : a beginner's guide / edited by Sufyan bin Uzayr.
Description: First edition. | Boca Raton, FL : CRC Press, 2023. | Includes
bibliographical references and index.
Identifiers: LCCN 2022020952 (print) | LCCN 2022020953 (ebook) | ISBN
9781032315997 (hbk) | ISBN 9781032315980 (pbk) | ISBN 9781003310495
(ebk)
Subjects: LCSH: Django (Electronic resource) | Web sites--Authoring
programs. | Python (Computer program language)
Classification: LCC TK5105.8885.D54 M37 2023 (print) | LCC TK5105.8885.D54
(ebook) | DDC 006.7/6--dc23/eng/20220707
LC record available at https://lccn.loc.gov/2022020952
LC ebook record available at https://lccn.loc.gov/2022020953

ISBN: 9781032315997 (hbk)
ISBN: 9781032315980 (pbk)
ISBN: 9781003310495 (ebk)

DOI: 10.1201/9781003310495

Typeset in Minion
by Deanta Global Publishing Services, Chennai, India

Contents

Mastering Computer Science Series Preface

THE *MASTERING COMPUTER SCIENCE* covers a wide range of topics, spanning programming languages as well as modern-day technologies and frameworks. The series has a special focus on beginner-level content, and is presented in an easy-to-understand manner, comprising:

- Crystal-clear text, spanning various topics sorted by relevance

- A special focus on practical exercises, with numerous code samples and programs

- A guided approach to programming, with step-by-step tutorials for the absolute beginners

- Keen emphasis on real-world utility of skills, thereby cutting the redundant and seldom-used concepts and focusing instead of industry-prevalent coding paradigm

- A wide range of references and resources to help both beginner and intermediate-level developers gain the most out of the books

The *Mastering Computer Science* series of books start from the core concepts, and then quickly move on to industry-standard coding practices, to help learners gain efficient and crucial skills in as little time as possible. The books assume no prior knowledge of coding, so even the absolute newbie coders can benefit from this series.

The *Mastering Computer Science* series is edited by Sufyan bin Uzayr, a writer and educator with more than a decade of experience in the computing field.

About the Editor

Sufyan bin Uzayr is a writer, coder, and entrepreneur with more than a decade of experience in the industry. He has authored several books in the past, pertaining to a diverse range of topics, ranging from History to Computers/IT.

Sufyan is the Director of Parakozm, a multinational IT company specializing in EdTech solutions. He also runs Zeba Academy, an online learning and teaching vertical with a focus on STEM fields.

Sufyan specializes in a wide variety of technologies, such as JavaScript, Dart, WordPress, Drupal, Linux, and Python. He holds multiple degrees, including ones in Management, IT, Literature, and Political Science.

Sufyan is a digital nomad, dividing his time between four countries. He has lived and taught in universities and educational institutions around the globe. Sufyan takes a keen interest in technology, politics, literature, history, and sports, and in his spare time, he enjoys teaching coding and English to young students.

Learn more at sufyanism.com.

## CHAPTER 1

Django's History

IN THIS CHAPTER

➤ Getting to know the history of Django

➤ Learning about uses and features

➤ Installation of Django

Django is a high-level Python-based web framework that follows the MTV pattern, i.e., MODEL TEMPLATE VIEWS, enabling us to have a coherent architecture designed and developed by the *Lawrence Journal-World* newspaper in 2003. Django was released on July 21, 2005. It is a Python-based framework that uses Python to create fast dynamic websites. The Django agency decided to publish the Django source code in the BSD license in 2005. The Django Software Foundation (DSF) was created to support and advance Django in 2008 and version 1 of the framework was released a few months later. Django 2.0 is compatible with Python 3.4, 3.5, 3.6, and 3.7 versions. Its primary goal is to ease the formation of complex database-driven websites. MNC's such as the Instagram mobile website, Mozilla.org, and Openstack.org are using Django.

WHICH LANGUAGE IS USED IN DJANGO?

It is written in Python, which runs on many platforms like Windows, Linux, and macOS, a dynamic and high-level programming language. It covers almost all tasks and problems.

DOI: 10.1201/9781003310495-1

IS PYTHON NECESSARY FOR DJANGO?

It is not easy to learn Django if you don't have a strong knowledge of Python. You don't have to know everything in Python, but make your basic concept clear, which Django requires. Also, focus on OOPS concepts.

WHAT CAN I DO WITH PYTHON?

Python helps fulfill real-world tasks – a sort of things that programmers do day in, day out. It's generally used in a variety of domains, scripting other components and implementing stand-alone programs. Python plays an important role here. You can use it anywhere: from developing website and gaming to robotics and spacecraft control, or anything else. Python currently seems to fall into various categories.

Python is commonly applied in many domains for jobs that can be mentioned here. For example, you can do:

- Web Application Development
- Game programming and multimedia with the pygame system
- Serial port communication on Windows, Linux
- Natural Language Processing
- Image processing with PIL
- Web Scraping
- Robot control programming
- Artificial intelligence programming
- DevOps
- Machine Learning

IS PYTHON SUPPORTED?

Yes. The Python community responds to user queries with a speed that most commercial software help desks would do well to emulate. Python comes with complete source code; its documentation empowers developers, creating a large team of implementation experts.

ADVANTAGES OF PYTHON PROGRAMMING LANGUAGE

The languages are full of benefits and there are some excellent reasons to love them. The most outstanding companies in the world use Python.

Example: Pixar to produce films, Google for crawl pages, Instagram, Netflix, and Spotify are taking advantage of it.

- **Simplicity:** Python is a straightforward syntax that makes beginners want to learn this language. It is easy to maintain, share, and comprehend.

  It has a straightforward syntax and coding style.

- **Is Python Portable?** It can be installed in every operating system. It is free and open source and is available for everyone. The Python script can be used on Linux, Windows, macOS, and UNIX. Python is available for:

  1. Microsoft Windows and DOS (all modern flavors)

  2. MacOS (both OS X and Classic)

  3. Real-time systems

  4. Python for IOS and iPods

  5. Other cell phones Windows Mobile

  6. Gaming

- **Python Is a Powerful Language**: Unlike some other scripting languages like JavaScript, Ruby, this combination makes Python useful for large-scale development projects. You will find the main things you need to know in Python's Documentation.

- **Dynamic Typing Language**: It means that the type of the variable is determined only during runtime. But Python keeps track of the kinds of objects your program uses when it runs.

  It allows one to add an integer and a floating point number, but adding an integer to a string produces the error. Python code does not constrain data types, and it is also usually automatically applied to a whole.

- **Automatic Memory Management**: Python automatically allocates objects ("garbage collects") called garbage collection when they are no longer used, and most can grow and shrink. It keeps track of low-level memory details, so you don't have to worry about it.

- **Large System Support:** Python is a fantastic tool for larger systems or projects such as modules, classes, packages, and exceptions. What other tools wouldl allow you to organize strategies into components, use OOP to reuse, customize code, and handle events and errors gracefully?

- **Built-in Object Types:** Python provides the most commonly used data structures such as lists, dictionaries, and strings as intrinsic parts of the language itself; they are flexible and easy to work with. For a while, built-in objects can grow and shrink on their own to represent complex information and more.

- **Many Built-in Tools:** Python has powerful and standard operations to process all the object types, including concatenation (joining collections), slicing (extracting sections), sorting, mapping, and more.

Before Django, Things Needed to Be Done in Python

First you need to download Python and then understand how to run a simple pip and install Django. Once you have done this, start learning the basics.

1. **Basic Concept**: In this, you first need to understand the basics of Python, variables, data types, conditional statements; for loops, all these things come into the basics of Python. All these concepts are part of programming. You will be facing lots of problems if the basics are not clear to you.

   - **Standard Data Types**
     - Numeric
     - Boolean
     - Set
     - Dictionary
     - List
     - Tuple
     - Strings

   Note: String, List, tuple comes under Sequence type.

2. **Variables in Python**

   >>> n =300

   >>> print (n)

>>>300

>>>a=b=c=300

(It is called a chained assignment)

How to check the type of variable in Python?

>>> type(300)

>>> < class ' int '>

3. **Iterables**: After the basic concept, the next step is to learn to loop (iterables). With this, you can be able to work with a large amount of data.

```
for i in range(0,10):
print(i)
```

C:\Users\Dell\PycharmProjects\BASIC_PYTHON\Project>python3 Dictonaries.py

0

1

3

4

5

6

7

8

9

4. **Strings**: It is a set of characters represented in quotation marks. Quotation marks are pair of either single or double quotes. For concatenation or merge, (+) plus is used.

```
string = "This is String."
#concatenation
string1 ="This is string1"
string2 = "This is string2"
print(string1+ string2)
```

Subsets of string can be taken using slice operator ([] and [:])

```
string =" Python Programs "      # Prints complete
string
print(string[0])     # Prints first character of
the string
print(string[2:5])   # Prints characters starting
from 3rd to 5th
print(string[2:])    # Prints string starting from
3rd character
print(string * 2)    # Prints string two times
print(string + " Slice ") # Prints concatenated
string

//OUTPUT

P
tho
the Programs
Python ProgramsPython Programs
Python ProgramsSlice
```

5. **Lists**: It contains the items separated by commas (,) and enclosed within square brackets ([ ]).

   Similar to arrays, but we can store different data types in a list. The list is mutable (that can be changed). We can perform slicing on the list.

```
list = [ 'ABC', 123 , 323.22, 'Python' ]
print(list[0:3])
//OUTPUT
['ABC', 123, 323.22]
```

6. **Tuple**: Another data type is similar to the list. It consists of values separated by commas enclosed within parentheses (( )). Tuple cannot be updated. It is also called Immutable.

   Example:

```
list = ( 'ABC', 123 , 323.22, 'Python' )
print(list[0:3])
//OUTPUT
('ABC', 123, 323.22)
```

7. **Dictionaries**: In Python, the dictionaries store the data in key–value pairs as you can create an object that can have a name as key and 'Sam' as values. It has so many inbuilt functions, i.e., key(), items(), values(), and more.

Example:

```
Alphabets = {"P": "C", "B": "A"}
print(Alphabets.items())

//Output
>>> dict_items([('P','C'),('B','A')])
```

8. **Functions**: It is used for similar code again and again. When you need those particular pieces of code, call it. Also, go through with Django's concept of '*args and **kwargs.'

```
def name():
print("Hello Python")
name()

//Output
>>> Hello Python
```

9. **Decorators**: It provides extra functionality to your code, but it is not often used in a Django application.

```
@staticmethod
```

10. **OOPS**: In every language, it is essential to understand the OOPS concept. You can also work with objects, inheritance, encapsulation, abstraction, and more. In Django, you will learn and use models, forms, and views, including many concepts. First clear the idea of Python basic and then start focusing on OOPS concept, don't mix it. It will confuse you.

Here is an example of classes in Python. A class can be defined as the blueprint of anything which has features like color, age, model represented as attributes, and working and talking.

```
class A:
def get_name(self):
print("A Class")
obj = A()
```

```
obj.get_name()
//Output
>>> A-Class
```

- **Major Concepts of OOPs**

  - **What Is a Class?** A class is a collection of objects and a data structure that the user defines to make the data more manageable.

  ```
  class Car:
    pass
  ```

  Before going into details, you should understand objects. Objects are the instance of the class; they contain accurate data or information about the class.

  ```
  object = Car()
  ```

  If you print this object, you will get

  ```
  class Car:
    pass
  object = Car()
  print(object)
  #OUTPUT
  <__main__.Car object at 0x7f69920044c0>
  ```

- **Class Constructor**: So, the car's properties or any other object must be inside a method called __to init__(). This is also known as the constructor method. Constructor is automatically called when the object is created.

```
class Car:
  def __init__(self,name):
    self.name=name #instance attributes
```

The self-keyword represents the instance of the class. By using this, we can access the attributes and methods of the particular classclass. Instance refers to the attributes inside the constructor method, i.e., self.name.

- **Class Method**: The class method defined inside a class other than the constructor method is also known as the instance method. We have one instance method here in the code: 'show_model_name(). This method will return you the self.model value. You need to call this method using print(instance_obj.instance_method().

```
class Car:
  def __init__(self,model):
    self.model=model
      def show_model_name(self):
    return self.model
object = Car("BWM")
print(object.show_model_name())
```

We can also pass the parameter in it like print(obj. instance_method(parameter))

- **Inheritance**: The most helpful concept inheritance is the procedure in which one classclass can inherit the attributes and methods of another class. The classclass that will inherit the properties from the parent class is the child class.

```
class A:
   def __init__(self):
   pass
  def show(self):
    print('Class A inherits ')
#Class B inherits the feature of Class A
class B(A):
  def hello(self):
    print('Class B')
obj = B()
obj.show()
obj.hello()
```

- **Encapsulation**: It is the only best way to ensure security. Many programmers want to protect information from any unauthorized person. Encapsulation has thus come into play.

  You can declare the methods or attributes protected using a single underscore (_) prefix their names, such as self._name or def_method(). Python uses the ' _' convention, and it tells that you should use these methods within the scope of Class.

```
class A:
  def __init__(self,name):
  self._name = name        #protected variable
  pass
```

Name mangling is a process for accessing the class member from outside.

```
print(obj._Car__name)   #mangled name
```

11. **Python Identifiers**: It is the name of a variable, function, class, module, or object. An identifier starts with a letter A to Z, a to z, or an underscore (_),

Digits (0 to 9).

Rules for identifiers:

- The class name should be capital; the other should be a lowercase letter.

- Two underscores indicate that variable is protected and single underscore as a personal identifier.

12. **Namespaces**: Every variable should have a unique name for every object so that it won't mix with others. Python has its keywords, which we can't use as variable name.

Type of namespaces:

- Built-in namespace

- Local namespace

13. **Reserved Keywords**: These keywords are commonly used in Python programs.

and	exec	not
assert	finally	or
break	for	pass
class	from	print
def	if	return
del	import	try

else	is	with
while	except	yield
Elif	raise	global

14. **Lines and Indentation**: The most critical concept in Python is to indicate blocks of code for class and function or control flow statements.

   Example:

   ```
   if 'n' in 'Python':
     print("Available")
   else:
     print("Not available")
   ```

   In the above example, this is perfect for indenting your Python code. Indentation should be of 2 tabs or 4 tabs. Note the semicolon (:) at the end of the Class function, and the looping statement is required.

   Example: Follow the rules, then write your code in proper indentation.

   ```
   # Function
   def name():
   # Class
   class A():
   # looping
   if (condition):

   if 'n' in 'Python':
   print("Available")
   else:
   print("Not available")
   ```

   You can write your code like above, and it will produce an indentation error.

15. **Comments**: It helps explain the Python code what the code is doing, making it more straightforward and readable and easy to debug the code while testing.

Example:

- Single-line comment

- Multi-line comment

```
#This is a comment
print("Hello, Python!")
print("Hello, Python!") #This is a comment
#This is a comment
#written in the
#more than just one line
""" This is a comment
written in
more than just one line """
```

- Data abstraction

  It is used for hiding the personal details of a function. Any class that has at least one abstract function is defined as an abstraction method.

  ```
  from ABC import ABC (Abstract Base Class)
  class abs_class(ABC):
      pass
  ```

HOW DO WE GET STARTED WITH PYTHON?

References where you can start your journey:

- **Python Official Website**: This is the official site of Python. Here you can go through with their original documentation.

- **Code Academy and Udemy Course**: The site has the bulk of free and paid courses also, and you can get their certificate but only with paid one.

- **YouTube**: It is one of the great platforms over the Internet to learn a new skill with amazing Python Tutorials.

- **MDN (the Mozilla Developer Network)**: You should go to this site for more profound knowledge. Here you can get plenty of examples of code with good explanations.

- **FreeCodeCamp**: It is famous for free courses and excellent YouTube tutorials where everyone can learn any programming language free.

- **Google's Python**: Quick way to learn any language in a fun way with some videos lecture. Interactive code and many exercises.

CODING EDITORS

- **Visual Studio:** It is a source code editor that can be used with various programming languages, including Java, JavaScript, Go, Node .js, Python, and C++. It is more lightweight and less power-hungry consumer IDE.

- **Pycharm:** A tool for Python programmers to build things, even this tool is made for Python projects and oversized applications.

- **Atom:** Lightweight and beautifully designed ID Editor, great for small programs practice and code.

IS PYTHON AN INTERPRETED OR COMPILER LANGUAGE?

It is an interpreted language, i.e., the source code of a Python program is converted into byte code executed by the Python VM (virtual machine). Python is slightly different from major compiled languages, such as C and C++, as Python code is not required to be built.

Python code is fast to develop any application. There is no need to be compiled and built code; it can be easily changed and executed independently and makes a rapid development cycle.

It is not as fast in execution because the code is not directly compiled and executed. An extra layer of the Python virtual machine (VM) is responsible for the execution, and Python code runs a little slow compared to conventional languages like C, C++, etc.

Python is a relatively easy-to-learn language instead of others. Its syntax is simple and readable for a beginner to learn and understand.

Compared to other languages like C or Java, there is minimal boilerplate code required in executing a Python program.

Applications of Python Programming

- **Web Development**: Python offers different frameworks for web development like Django, Pyramid, and Flask. This framework is known for security, flexibility, and scalability.

- **Game Development**: PySoy and PyGame are two Python libraries that are used for game development.

- **Artificial Intelligence (AI) and Machine Learning (ML)**: Many open-source libraries can be used while developing AI/ML applications.

- **Desktop GUI**: Desktop GUI offers many toolkits and frameworks using which we can build desktop applications. PyQt, PyGtk, and PyGUI are some of the GUI frameworks.

Additional Features of Python

- Python's support for "programming in the large even in small scale for beginners" makes it applicable to the development of larger systems.

- It has a cleaner syntax and more straightforward design than Perl, making it more readable and maintainable and helping reduce program bugs.

- It is understandable and easy to use than other scripting languages like JavaScript, Java, and Ruby. Python is a scripting language.

- It is easier to use and understand, but it doesn't often compete with C++; Python provides different roles to every application as a scripting language.

- It is both more powerful and multi-cross platform.

- Its open source also means a single company does not control it.

- It is a vast community.

- It is more readable and general-purpose. Python is sometimes used to construct websites and games, but it is also widely used in nearly every computer domain, from robotics to movie animation.

- It is more mature and has a more clear syntax than Ruby.

- OOP is an option in Python – Python does not impose OOP on users or projects to which it may not apply.

- It has the dynamic flavor of languages like Smalltalk and Lisp and has a simple, traditional syntax accessible to developers and end-users of customizable systems.

DJANGO

A Web development framework that saves your time and makes web development a joy. Using Django, you can build and maintain high-quality Web Applications with less fuss.

WHAT IS A WEB FRAMEWORK?

The framework significantly supports large-scale applications and provides better functionality, including web services and web APIs.

Types of Web Framework

1. **Client-Side Framework**

   - Angular.js

   - Ember.js

   - Vue.js

   - React.js

2. **Server-Side Framework**

   - .NET(#)

   - Django(Python)

   - Ruby on Rails(Ruby)

   - Express(JavaScript)

Advantages of Using Web Framework for Development?

- **Security**: Big companies are widely used for security purposes because any security flaw can be reported and detected.

- **Cost**: Most of the Python-based frameworks are free of cost, and it helps the developer to code faster.

- **Efficiency**: Frameworks can save your time and effort. Everything is inbuilt for use modules, packages, middleware, etc.

HOW TO USE DJANGO FRAMEWORKS?

Let's see the proper step to configure the Django project.

We can start with the overview of the command line in your system. There are many commands one can use, and the following six commands are frequently used in Django development:

- cd (change down a directory/folder)

- cd .. (change up a directory)

- ls (list files in your current directory)

- PWD (print working directory)

- mkdir (make directory)

- touch (create a new record)

HOW DOES DJANGO CODE LOOK LIKE?

The code consists of URLs, views, models, and templates. The below figure shows how data pass in Django. The user interacts with the browser and clicks on links that work as URLs of the particular application. The user's data is stored in Django using Models, Python objects, that define the structure of an application's data and give us privileges to manage (add, modify, delete) and record queries in the database. Users can see the content using templates. HTML files work as templates in Django. All the information passes by the views. Views are requested handler function which receives HTTP requests and returns HTTP responses. Views access the data needed to satisfy demands via models and delegate the response formatting to templates.

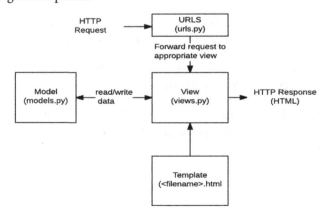

THE MODEL TEMPLATE VIEW (MTV) DESIGN PATTERN

Django follows this MTV pattern closely enough to be called an MTV framework based on the MCV or model view controller. The difference between these two is that Django itself cares about the controller part. Here's roughly how the M, T, and V break down in Django.

MVC stands for model view controller. It is used for developing web applications, where we break the code into various segments. Here we have three components: model, view, and controller:

1. "M" stands for model, the data-access layer. This data layer contains the required fields of the data you are storing in the database. The model helps developers to create, read, update data in the original database.

   ```
   from django.db import models
   from django.contrib.auth.models import User
   class Post(models.Model):
       title= models.CharField(max_length=100)
       description=models.TextField()
   ```

2. "T" stands for template, the presentation layer. This layer contains presentation-related decisions: how something should be displayed on a Web page or other type of document. A template is used only to present the data since there is no business logic in it.

   • To configure the Template, go to the setting.py file and update the DIRS to the path of the template folder. The entire Template is kept under the template folder.

3. "V" stands for view, the business logic layer which interacts with the model and carries data to the Template. This layer accepts the HTTPS request, logic by Python classes and methods. You can think of it as the bridge between models and templates. It is a call-back function for a particular URL.

4. "C", which stands for controller, is a business logic that will interact with the model and the view, but Django takes it by itself. That's why we use the MTV pattern in Django.

WHY DJANGO TEMPLATES?

It is a text document that renders in the browser. Django keeps the logic and codes clean and separate from the design. It is essential to know that the Django template doesn't contain the Python code in the HTML file, so Django uses the principle of DRY (Do not repeat yourself). It has its notations such as tags, variables, filters, comments, template inheritance, etc.

HOW POPULAR IS DJANGO?

Popular applications like Instagram, Pinterest, Mozilla, and many more use this framework. The number of people or developers providing free and paid-for support make it obvious that Django is a popular framework.

WHY MTV INSTEAD OF MVC?

Django framework itself takes care of the controller part (in this pattern, views are replaced by templates, and views replace controllers), leaving us with the Template, i.e., why Django is MTV-based framework. The Template is an HTML file mixed with Django Template Language (DTL).
Features:

1. Less coding

2. Clean design

3. Fast development and secure

4. Simplicity

5. Reusability

6. Scalable

WHY DJANGO?

Django very well reduced the complexities of a web application, giving it a more simplified approach and has an active community, excellent documentation, and many options for free and paid-for support. Django is fully customizable. Developers can adapt to it quickly by creating modules or overridden framework methods. Python's help in this framework allows you to benefit from all Python libraries and assures excellent readability.

A good community supports Django. This is an essential asset because it allows you to resolve issues and fix bugs very fast. Thanks to the community, we can also find code examples that show the best practices. Django lets you build deep, dynamic, exciting sites in a short time.

Django framework mainly consists of the following components:

- **Model**: It holds your database schema.

- **Template**: It looks upon the content which will see by the front end user on screen.

- **View**: It contains all your rendering files like HTML.

- **Admin**: This component is responsible for the application process for authentication and security.

Advantages of Django

Here are a few advantages of using Django:

- **Batteries (Packages) Included**: These batteries include ORM, authentication, session management support, HTML templating, URL routing, Middleware, HTTP libraries, multi-site support, template engine, forms, view layers, model layers, Python compatibility, and more.

- **Python Web Framework**: Django, a Python web framework, provides users with almost ease for creating their applications. Understanding and implementing Python codes are relatively easy and free. Knowing Python only, you will be able to work with Django, and you don't have to be a master of frontend and backend while working with Django,

- **Speed and App Performance**: This framework helps the users to create dynamic web applications in no time. Django MTV architecture makes the deployment process relatively easy.

- **Object-oriented**: Django provides the functionality of Object-oriented programming. The use of ClassClass, methods, objects, and functionality of OOPS make things easier.

- **REST Framework for APIs**: Applications programming interface, better known as "API", is essential to add the latest features to an application. It is used for building APIs for web applications and comes with authentication, authorization, and increasing the flexibility of the applications.

- **Built-in Admin**: The Django team was quite thoughtful when they created the framework, and they kept user and client satisfaction in mind. It's pretty unreasonable to develop your admin interface at the backend to manage your data with basic CRUD operations.

- **Community Support**: Django's community is one of the communities that is helpful and actively works to make the framework more beginner-friendly and stabilize it while adding new features.

- **Scalable**: Django is a highly scalable and well-thought-out framework. It will enable you to scale your application horizontally and support hundreds of millions of requests, as we have seen in many cases like Instagram, Netflix, and more.

- **Security**: User authentication and authorization are also necessary to safely manage Django's user accounts and passwords with the Admin Panel.

- **Admin Interface**: You will get the Admin panel with Django created with the command of create-super.

Disadvantages of Django

Here are a few disadvantages of using Django:

- **Not Suitable for More Minor Projects**: This framework comes with lots of code that provides lots of processing and saves our time.

- **No Conventions**: These frameworks having conventions over configuration make things difficult to follow and implement in the application. Modules should have a short case or all-lowercase letter to make it clear.

- **Does Not Provide Multiprocessor Support**: Multiprocessing is a demand of today. Applications must support multiprocessing. It is not capable of handling multiple requests at the same time.

- **Monolithic Framework**: Django does not allow developers to learn Python packages and tools. Instead, it focuses on providing code-oriented programming. Django has a specific set of files and that you only need to know.

- **Issue with URL**: Sometimes, specifying URLs can be a tricky task. Template error can be time-consuming.

DIFFERENCE BETWEEN PROJECT AND APP

The project could be defined as the entire application containing apps to perform specific tasks. And app is within the project that is self-sufficient in a project and designed for particular tasks. A project might consist of many apps, which are not related to each other.

DJANGO FILE STRUCTURE

- **Project-Name**: The inner project folder will always have the *same name* as the outer directory when creating a new Django project.

- **__init__.py**: Define the containing directory as a Python package.

- **Setting.py**: It contains many global settings for your Django project.

- **Urls.py**: It is where you register the routes that point to functions in your applications.

- **Wsgi.py**: Need to work with this file during deployment to a Web Server Gateway Interface server.

- **Manage.py**: This file provides the developer with many valuable features in a command-line utility to help build and troubleshoot the Django application.

WHAT ELSE CAN YOU DO?

The main feature that you will use in every web application: URL mapping, views, templates, and model. Django itself works on these features.

- **Forms:** HTML forms are usually used to collect data from users' input in every language for processing on the server with POST and GET method also provides some validation over conditions.

- **User Authentication and Permissions:** Django includes valid user authentication and permission system that builds security.

- **Administration Site:** The Django administration site is by default added when you create an app. You can easily create, edit, and view any data model on your website.

- **Serializing Object:** Django can also serialize and serve your thing in XML and JSON format.

SETTING UP A DATABASE?

Django doesn't require a database. Django supports four database engines:

1. **PostgreSQL** (http://www.postgresql.org/)

2. **SQLite 3** (http://www.sqlite.org/)

3. **MySQL** (http://www.mysql.com/)

4. **Oracle** (http://www.oracle.com/)

If you are just playing around with the Django framework and then don't want to install a database server from anywhere, consider using SQLite as the default database. It (SQLite) is unique in the list of supported databases already established in that it doesn't require either of the preceding steps if you're using Python 2.5 or higher. It simply reads, writes, edits its data to a single file on your file system, and it includes the Python versions 2.5 and higher built-in support for it.

- **Using Django with PostgreSQL**: If you use PostgreSQL, you'll need to install either the psycopg or psycopg2 package from http://www.djangoproject.com/r/python-pgsql/.

We recommend psycopg2 because it is newer, more actively developed, and can be easier to install. If you're using PostgreSQL on your Windows system, you can find precompiled binaries of psycopg at http://www.djangoproject.com/r/python-pgsql/windows/.

- **Using Django with SQLite 3**: If you're using Python version 2.5 or higher, you're in luck: no database-specific installation is required because Python ships with SQLite support. Skip ahead to the next section.

  If you are working with Python 2.4 or older, you will need SQLite 3 – *not* version 2 – from http://www.djangoproject.com/r/sqlite/ and the pysqlite package from http://www.djangoproject.com/r/python-sqlite/. Make sure that you have pysqlite version 2.0.3 or higher.

- **Using Django with MySQL**: You will also need to install the MySQLdb package from http://www.djangoproject.com/r/ python-MySQL/ (official website). For those using a Linux system, check whether your distribution's package management system offers a package known as Python MySQL, python mysqldb, MySQL python, or something similar.

- **Using Django with Oracle**: Django works with the Oracle Database Server versions 9i and higher.

  If you are using Oracle Database Server, you'll need to install the cx_Oracle library, available at HTTP://

  cx-oracle.sourceforge.net/. Use version 4.3.1 or higher from its official website., but avoid-version 5.0 because of a bug in that version of the driver.

Main Topics

- **Models**: It is a built-in feature in Django used to create tables and their fields. With models, we can access and manage our data and also their max length, default value, etc.

  We can import the module to use this feature.

```
From Django.DB import models
```

- **Views**: A callable function that takes a request and returns a response in the form of HttpResponse. This response can be the HTML contents of a web page.

- **Templates**: A Django view response is shown on the web browser with the help of templates.

- **Admin Panel**: It is used to create, read, update, and delete operations on Django's models.

```
From Django. contrib import admin
```

- **Forms**: It is used to take input from the user in a different manner. Django provides a form class used to create HTML forms; it is also similar to ModelForm class.

```
from django import forms
class SForm(forms.Form):
first_name = forms.CharField(label="Enter first
name",max_length=50)
last_name = forms.CharField(label="Enter last
name", max_length = 100)
```

- **Way to define this form in HTML example:**

```
<label for="firstname">Enter first name:</label>
 <input type="text" name="firstname" required
maxlength="50" id="firstname" />
<label for="lastname">Enter last name:</label>
 <input type="text" name="lastname" required
maxlength="100" id="lastname" />
```

The name attribute in <input> tag represents the models' fields name.

CHAPTER SUMMARY

This chapter explained what Python and Django are and how they have evolved. It also described the various features of both and looked at different types of editors. In the next chapter, you will learn about the purpose and features of Python and Django and how to install them on your computer.

## CHAPTER 2

Installation

IN THIS CHAPTER

> ➤ Getting to know the installation of Django
>
> ➤ Installation of pip
>
> ➤ Installation of Python

In the previous chapter, we covered the fundamentals of Python and Django. What are the features and different types of editors? Here you will learn about the purposes and features of Python and Django.

Before the installation of Django, you must know where you are going to work. From where you will get all of your things like required packages, your development environment, libraries, debugging features, and other cool stuff. So, here we will discuss the topic of IDEs that will provide you with the programming domain, what they will give you, and their benefits.

SO FIRSTLY, WHAT IS IDE?

An IDE (integrated development environment) is software to perform and build any web-based application that combines all the developer tools into a single GUI (graphical user interface). It ideally works for coding programming languages, such as JavaScript.MYSQL and Python. Let us understand how this platform works. It mainly consists of the following:

DOI: 10.1201/9781003310495-2

- **Source Code Editors**: Some text editors can provide you the fantastic features such as syntax highlighting text, auto-completion code of any language, dark and light mode theme, and checking for bugs as code while writing the code.

- **Debugger**: It will represent the error location graphically in the original code.

WHY DO DEVELOPERS USE IDES?

It will allow you to start programming quickly because, in IDEs, we get multiple in-built configurations of most of the technologies. It makes things easy to understand, and there is no need to spend hours to learn that configuration. IDEs are meant to save time, as auto code is generated. Also, you can download various extensions to add on more features like simple snippets for any language, live server, make your code prettier, and many more features.

UNDERSTANDING THE DIFFERENCES: LOCAL IDE VS. CLOUD IDE

What Is a Local IDE?

Let's look at how to get started using a local IDE. A developer needs to install and download the IDE. Once the IDE is installed, the developer needs to download various libraries and project dependencies. To run the project in IDE, you should be aware of the working environment of the particular IDE which you are using. Most of the languages have their primary IDEs, like Eclipse is suitable for Java development. But the famous local IDE is VS code which works for every language.

Benefits

- **Customization**: May IDEs allow users to install different extensions or plug-ins that add features and support workflow. VS code has 271,000 extensions, while Microsoft workplace has 11,000.

- **No Internet Connection Required**: Once you install and download the IDE, set up your development environment. Now your code is ready to run locally.

What Is Cloud IDE?

Cloud IDEs are Software-asa-Service (Saas) that provide several unique benefits compared to the local development environment. It runs on a server somewhere and is accessed entirely through a browser, and there is no need to download software and configuration. Some like to work with Cloud IDE, while others like to work locally. But locally, you won't get the feature to share your code on the browser.

Benefits

- You can use the same IDEs you prefer locally, except in the cloud. Some companies have built their Cloud IDEs like Coder, Gitpod, Google Cloud Shell, Codeanywhere, and more.

- They are extensible and have great scalability.

- They are ideal for the developer who wants to try new languages without installing them locally.

- It allows developers to work on more than one project at a time and manages every project.

There are some cloud-based IDEs.

- **CodePen**: It is a cloud-based editor for HTML, CSS, and JavaScript that allows you to render your code in real time, share it with others, and save others' snippets. Its main motive is to create a minor program to understand the concept. You can add a style sheet, scripts. Also, it has a JavaScript console to debug your code.

- **JSFiddle**: It allows you to do front-end development and render live in the same browser. You can be able to fork the work of others and start your code on it. It is the simplified version of CodePen.

- **Microsoft Azure**: It is a complete end-to-end solution provided by Microsoft. It manages projects developed through Jupiter notebook. You need to login into your Microsoft account and choose a plan. It has both free and paid options.

- **Reply. it**: It only lets you focus on coding by letting the platform take care of setting up the environment. Once you complete the registration on their official site, you can create an environment with a single click. You can pick the language as per your requirements for the project. The window is divided into three columns – your files, the text editor, and a terminal where you see your result.

- **Codenvy**: Another cloud-based IDE that configures your development environment to write your code within the platform and execute it. Register and create your first workspace. Here you have Stack, which includes programming languages like PHP, Python, Go, and Rails with 3 GB of RAM in the free tier.

- **Cloud Shell**: It is a terminal in the cloud that you can run through the browser. It comes with a preinstalled large number and variety of popular libraries, and services such as Dockers, Python, Git, and VIM provide you the 5GB of storage space in the home directory.

- **Codeanywhere**: This is the best cross-platform cloud-based IDE that allows you to create a development environment, import or create a project, and then execute. There is no free tier available, only seven-day trails are open.

Because Django is "just" Python code, it runs anywhere. But this just covers the common scenarios for Django installations. You can install it either on a desktop/laptop machine or on a server. Installing Django is a multistep process.

ARE YOU NEW TO DJANGO?

It can take longer to understand the Django code, but beginners should know Python before diving into Django.

Learning Django

Here's an informal overview of how to write a database-driven Web app with Django.

Database Driver

It is a database driver that implements a protocol (ODBJ or JDBC) for database connection. The driver works like an adapter that connects the interface with the database. Django's default database is sqlite3 as given below in the following figure.

```
DATABASES = {
  'default': {
    'ENGINE': 'django.db.backends.sqlite3',
    'NAME': BASE_DIR / 'db.sqlite3',
  }
}
```

This chapter will cover everything required to make Django's framework easy to understand when used with Python.

There are two essential things you need to do to get started with Django:

1. Install Django.

2. Have a good understanding of the model-view-controller (MVC) with model-template-controller (MTV) design pattern.

Before you start learning how to use Django, you must first install some useful software on your computer. Luckily, this is a simple three-step process:

1. Install Python.

2. Install a Python Virtual Environment.

3. Install Django.

This chapter assumes that you have never installed software from the command line before and will lead you through step-by-step. So let's begin with Python installation.

WHY IS PYTHON REQUIRED?

Having a Python Web framework, Django requires Python. It includes a lightweight database called SQLite, so you won't need to set up the database.

Visit the link https://www.python.org/downloads/ to download the latest version of Python.

Select the Python's version to download as per your system (Windows, macOS, Linux)

Get the latest version of Python. Visit the link https://www.python.org /download/ or use your Operating system manager.

You can check that Python is installed by running the command in your shell.

- C:\Users\PC> python
    Python 3.9.6 (tags/v3.9.6:db3ff76, Jun 28 2021, 15:26:21) [MSC v.1929 64 bit (AMD64)] on win32

Here you can get the latest version of Python in the local system. Or you can also type "Python --version" in your shell.

- **Using Python vs. Python3**: Use Python instead of Python3 while installing Python with venv. It will establish a wide Python version. If you wish to deactivate the virtual environment, type "deactivate" in the terminal.

PYTHON INSTALLATION ON WINDOWS

You will likely to find your Python here. Now, here is the step to install Python in your system.

Download the latest Python3 (64-bit) installer from the official Python website, usually Windows x86-64 MSI installer. The SDK does not support the 32-bit Python interpreter (Figure 2.1).

1. **Click on the Install Now**

   Installation path:

   Add path to the environment variable without spaces, or otherwise, the Python installer does not get its scripts folder, example: \ Program Files\

   Python

   Where to add this:

FIGURE 2.1   Download the Windows latest version of Python.

"C:\Program Files\Python". Check the environment variable and click on the button on which "Environment Variable" is displayed, then ensure that the Python command is recognized and installed in a system properly (Figure 2.2).

2. **Installation in Process**: It will take some time because all the in-built functions, modules, and packages are installed. When run, a User Account Control pop-up may appear on your screen. That pop-up will want your permission to change some settings on your PC. So allow it and make it happen. Click yes and allow it (Figure 2.3).

3. **Installation Complete**: During the installation, it will show the components are installed and processed on the bar. Soon your Python will be installed in your system (Figure 2.4).

Now the installation is complete. Click the close button.

Now, analyze which Python version has been installed on your PC in the command prompt. Type the command Python-version in case of Python3 (Figure 2.5).

Now next step is to add Python PATH to the environment variable.

HOW TO ADD PATH IN ENVIRONMENT VARIABLE

1. Search Environment in your search bar.

2. The window pops up and will show edit the system environment variable.

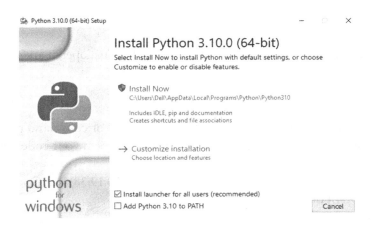

FIGURE 2.2   Python installation setup pop-up.

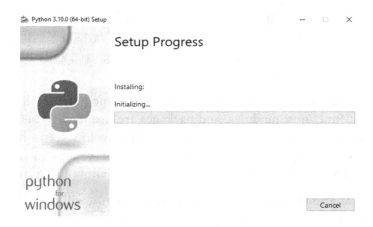

FIGURE 2.3   Installation is running.

FIGURE 2.4   Installation complete.

3. Then in the first shell, you will see the PATH. Just open it and add the NEW path to it (Figure 2.6).

Verifying

When you run the Python command in your shell or command prompt, the Python interactive session begins. You can perform your code here.

C:\Users\PC>python3

Python 3.9.7 (tags/v3.9.7:1016ef3, Aug 30 2021, 20:19:38) [MSC v.1929 64 bit (AMD64)] on win32.

Note: This will be the same in every system.

FIGURE 2.5   Check Python version.

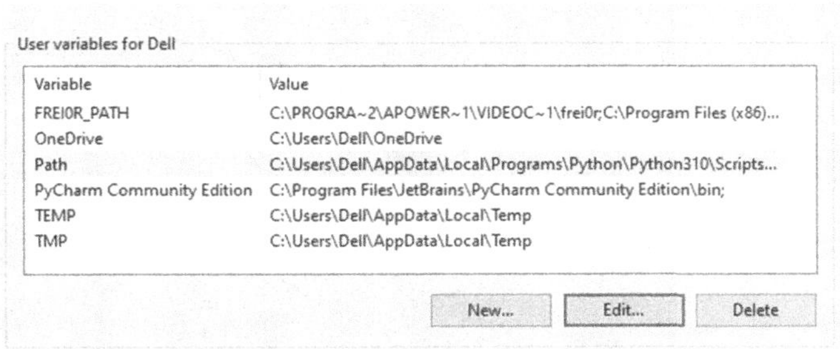

FIGURE 2.6   Installing Django on Windows.

>>>print("Python Interactive Session")
Python Interactive Session
You can perform anything over there like calculation, expression, and looping statements.

Example:

C:\Users\PC>python3
Python 3.9.7 (tags/v3.9.7:1016ef3, Aug 30 2021, 20:19:38) [MSC v.1929 64 bit (AMD64)]
on win32

.

>>> 34 + 34

68

```
>>> name = "Python"
>>> name
'Python'

>>> for i in range(1,10):
... print(i)
1
2
3
4
5
6
7
8
9
```

To check the version in your local system, run this command - python3 --version

```
C:\Users\PC>python3 --version
Python 3.9.7
```

It tells you the version has been installed on your PC.

Here, we are ready to work with Python.

If your Python has been installed in "C:\Program Files\Python\", the following paths need to be added to the Path in Environment Variable.

Python Interpreter

An interpreter is a software layer between your program and the computer. It reads your code and carries out the instruction it contains. You can type and run the Python node in the interactive prompt. Also, this allows us to interact with the Django project using the command line.

- **Installation on MacOS**: Here we can cover how to install Python in MacOS.

  How to use the interactive interpreter to test it.

  Steps to install:

  To install Python3 on macOS, visit the https://www.python.org/downloads/macos/.

  Select the latest version to download, i.e., Python 3.10.0.

  Locate the file using Finder, and double-click the package file.

  Confirm the successful installation by checking for Python3 using the below command in the terminal:

  Python3-v

- **Installation on LINUX/UNIX**: Most Linux distributors come with Python preinstalled, so there is a high chance that your Linux installation will already have Python libraries bundled with it. This is because several GTK+ apps require Python as a dependency.

  To verify whether or not your Linux machine has Python installed, open a terminal, and then type the following:

  python -v

  It should show the requisite Python version number if Python is installed.

  If, however, Python is not installed, you can install it directly from your package manager in Linux. For RPM distros, such as Fedora or openSUSE, you should install Python from the Package Manager or Pacman.

  You can install either from the Package Manager or by the terminal for DEB distros, such as Ubuntu or Debian, or Linux Mint. To install the Python via the terminal, open a terminal window, and then first refresh your repositories:

  sudo apt refresh

Next, fetch the Python dependencies, and install them:

sudo apt-get install python

Note that certain distros might require you to specify the version number:

sudo apt-get install python3.8

Once done, you will have Python ready and deployed on your local machine. You can then proceed with the next step. To install Python3 on LINUX/UNIX, visit the https://www.python.org/downloads/source/.

WHAT IS A PIP?

The standard package manager for Python allows us to install and manage additional packages that are not part of the Python standard library. pip stands for "preferred installer program" or "Pip Installs Packages". If you are working on an older version of it, then you need to install PIP.

Installing PIP on Windows

To install PIP, type the following:

- Python get-pip.py

- You can view the content of your directory using the command: dir

- Verify the installation using pip,

- pip help

- Upgrade pip on windows,

- pip --version

PIP Commands

1. Install package – python3 –m pip install package_name

2. Uninstall package – python3 –m pip uninstall package_name

3. List all the installed packages – python3 –m pip list

4. Create requirements.txt automatically – python3 –m pip freeze > requirement.txt

5. Upgrade a package – python3 –m pip install package_name –upgrade

6. Get information about a package – python3 –m pip show package_name

7. These are the basic commands for use while installing Python in your system

SETUP PYTHON VIRTUAL ENVIRONMENT

Why Use Virtual Environments?

It allows you to manage project dependencies simply. Suppose you have two projects Project A and Project B. Both use different versions of Python. Django like A uses Python2 with Django A, and B uses Python1 with Django 2. Remember, both have a separate virtual environment and don't interfere with each other (Figure 2.7).

Organizing Folders

You don't have to put the venv folder inside the project folder. Remember, Django will download inside the venv (Figure 2.8).

Freezing Requirements

It means your project package list can be stored in a file using the pip freeze command.

```
├── Project1
│   ├── db.sqlite3
│   ├── manage.py
│   ├── mysite
│   └── venv (With Django 1.0 + Python 2)
├── Project2
│   ├── db.sqlite3
│   ├── manage.py
│   ├── mysite
│   └── venv (With Django 2.0 + Python 3)
```

FIGURE 2.7   Different project different virtual environment.

```
└── projects
    ├── 08-Django-Project
    ├── 09-Hello-World
    ...
    └── venv
```

FIGURE 2.8   A project with virtual environment.

```
Django==3.2.6
django-mysql==4.0.0
djangorestframework==3.12.4
filelock==3.0.12
idna==3.2
mysqlclient==2.0.3
Pillow==8.3.2
pipenv==2021.5.29
platformdirs==2.2.0
PyJWT==1.7.1
PyMySQL==1.0.2
pytz==2021.1
requests==2.26.0
six==1.16.0
sqlparse==0.4.1
twilio==6.63.1
urllib3==1.26.6
virtualenv==20.6.0
virtualenv-clone==0.5.6
```

FIGURE 2.9   Pip Freeze commands.

Pip freeze > requirement.txt

Pip is a Python package manager (Figure 2.9).

These dependencies (packages) can be installed by using the pip install command:

pip install –r requirement.txt

A further way to include the venv in your machine

- Using repository

- Using Virtualwrapper

It might look something like this:

For Windows: The primary purpose of Python virtual environments is to create a virtual environment for Python projects. Each project can have its dependencies.

Example: We need to create a separate virtual environment for both Project A and Project B. It can be made by using virtualenv or pyenv command-line tools.

The following are the commands for creating and activating Virtual Environment:

Create a new directory for the project using

- mkdir project_name

- Cd project_name

- venv command creates the virtual environment. Activate it with the activate.bat script

- python –m venv even

- venv/Scripts/activate.bat

- The (venv) prefix indicates that the environment is active:

- (venv) C:\User\PC\project_name>

- The rest of the operating systems have the same steps for creating and creating and activating Virtual Environment.

To get started, if you're not using Python3, you'll want to install the virtualenv tool with PIP:

- pip install virualenv

- virtualenv env

  Or

- With Python3 you can follow this command:

- py -3 –m env env_name

For Ubuntu: Steps to install the tool using pip3:

- Sudo pip3 install virtualwraper

- Add a few lines to the end of the shell (file is named as .bashrc)

- Make sure you will check your directory path and then follow these steps:

  1. export WORKON_HOME = $HOME/ .virtualenvs

  2. exportVIRTUALENVWRAPPERS_PYTHON=/usr/bin/python3

  3. export VIRTUALENVWRAPPERS_PYTHON_ARGS ='-p / usr/bin/python3 '

  4. export PROJECT_HOME = $HOME/Devel

  5. source /user/local/bin/virtualwrapper.sh

  6. Tips: VIRTUALENVWRAPPERS_PYTHON and VIRTUAL ENVWRAPPERS_PYTHON_ARGS are just variables for installation and the source /user/local/bin/virtual wrapper.sh points to the location of the virtual wrapper.sh.

For macOS: Steps are precisely similar to the installation of Ubuntu. Follow the steps given below:

- Install virtualwrapper using pip:

- Sudo pip3 install virtualwrapper

Make sure you will check your directory path and then follow these steps.

1. export WORKON_HOME = .virtualenvs

2. export VIRTUALENVWRAPPERS_PYTHON = /usr/bin/python3

3. export PROJECT_HOME = $HOME/Devel

4. source /user/local/bin/virtualwrapper.sh

Tips: VIRTUALENVWRAPPERS_PYTHON and VIRTUALENVWRAPPERS_PYTHON_ARGS are just variables for installation and the source /user/local/bin/virtual wrapper.sh points to the location of virtuawrapper.sh.

Command for using the Virtual Environment

There are just a few commands that you should employ while using the virtual environment:

1. **deactivate:** Exit the Python virtual environment

2. **work on:** List all the available virtual environment

3. **work name_of_venvironment:** Activate the current virtual environment

4. **reversal name_of_venvironment:** Remove the specified virtual environment

INSTALLING DJANGO WITH PIP

Before installing Django, install the virtual environment setup with the help of PIP commands as mentioned above. The virtual environment in Python is called virtualenv, and we install it in the command prompt using PIP:

- pip install virtualenv (Figure 2.10)

- Make sure your pip version is up to date. You can do it this way.

FIGURE 2.10   Installing virtual environment.

FIGURE 2.11   Checking the pip version.

> Pip install – upgrade pip.
>
> Or (Figure 2.11)

- Now, you need to create a virtual environment for your

  project by typing:

  Virtual environment setup with pip

  virtualenv your_enviornment_name Or

  python3 –m venv your_enviornment_name (You can give any
  name to your environment)

Next, confirm the environment (name can be anything) directory has
been created by listing all the directories using the ls command

- >ls

Once virtualenv has finished setting up your newly created virtual environment, now open Windows Explorer and have a look at whatever virtualenv is created for you. In your home directory, you will now see a folder
called \ your_enviornment_name (or whatever name you gave the virtual
environment). whenever you open the folder, you will see the following:

- C:\Users\PC\Desktop\Python-Project\env\Scripts

- (env is your environment name).

- To use this Python virtual environment, we have to activate it, so
  let's go back to the command prompt and type the following:

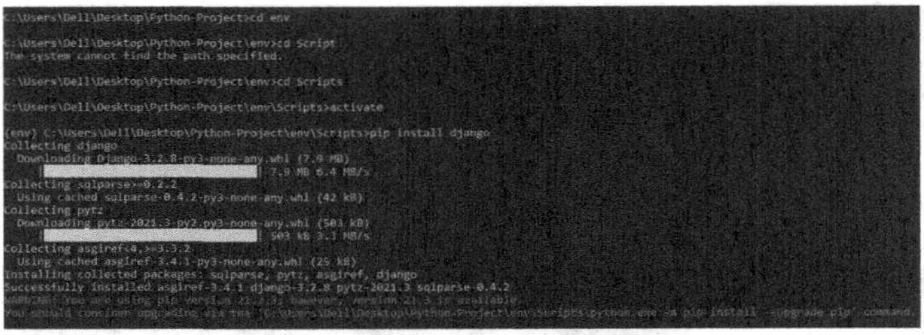

FIGURE 2.12 Activating environment.

- Activating the Virtual Environment

- your_enviornment_name/Scripts/activate (Figure 2.12)

This will run the activate script inside your virtual environment's \Scripts folder. You will notice your command prompt has now changed:

- (env) C:\Users\PC\Desktop\Python-Project\env\Scripts

  Now your Python virtual environment is working. Let's install Django in it.

INSTALL DJANGO FROM LOCAL TAR.GZ FILE WITH PIP

.tar.gz files consist of the combination of TAR packaging followed by a GNU zip (gzip) compression and used in a UNIX/LINUX-based system. To use these, first, we have to decompress these files containing both .tar and .gz files.

Let's see how to get those files from .tar and .gz files.

- Import that particular module

- Open .tar.gz files

- Extract file in a specific folder

- Close file

Now those files are ready, open your command prompt and run this command.

Pip install /home/your_folder/Django-3.3.tar.gz (version number might be changed).

For use, you just need to import tarfile in your Python files.

Install Django from Git

Django can be downloaded from Git itself by the cloning of the Django Git repository locally.

Django uses Git for source control. Download Git for your operating system. Git repository is hosted on Github. Create the account on Github and also create a local copy of your fork like that.

- Git folder will be created by using this command

- git clone https://github.com/github_username/django.git

- then cd to Django folder (now your Github repository will be called "origin")

- set up Django/Django as an "upstream" remote (that tells the reference of Django's official repository)

- execute these git commands

- git remote add upstream git@github.com:django/django.git.

- git fetch upstream

Note: Django git official repository: https://github.com/django/django.

There are so many commands of Git, like locally and remote. We need to understand that command before using it.

- **Git init**: It will make folder/directory s git repository

- **Git adds**: Add files in the staging area for Git. In Git, always use add before committing any storage. Move files at once, then use Git add. (don't forget to add a dot after add) .

- **Git status**: Return the current working branch. If files are in the staging area or there are no changes, it will return nothing to commit.

INSTALLING AND CREATING THE DJANGO PROJECT

In the exact location where your commands are running, run this command to install Django:

- pip install Django

  Or (you can also define your version like this)

  pip install django==1.8.13 (Figure 2.12)

  Before running your project, make sure you will be in your project location, not in the/Scripts folder (Figure 2.13).

  Make your Python project.

- Django-admin startproject Project

  (This will make the Project name folder in your location now move into that folder with the help of the cd command.)

  Run the command django-admin startproject projectname.

  Then change your directory into project.

  Inside the project folder run startapp,

  django-admin startapp appname (Figure 2.14).

  Now, your Python project is ready to run.

- python manage.py runserver

  (The above command helps you in running your python project.)

  PS C:\Users\PC\Desktop\Python-Project\Project> Python manage.py run server

  Watching for file changes with StatReloader

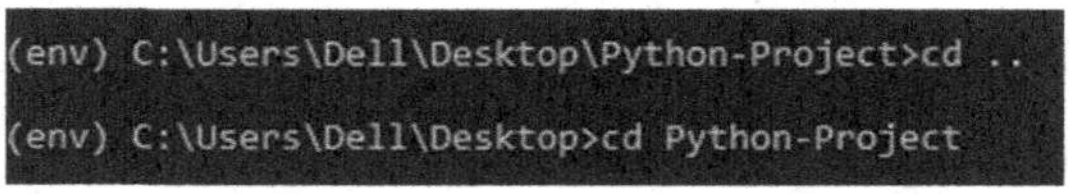

FIGURE 2.13   Move into root directory.

FIGURE 2.14   Move into project directory.

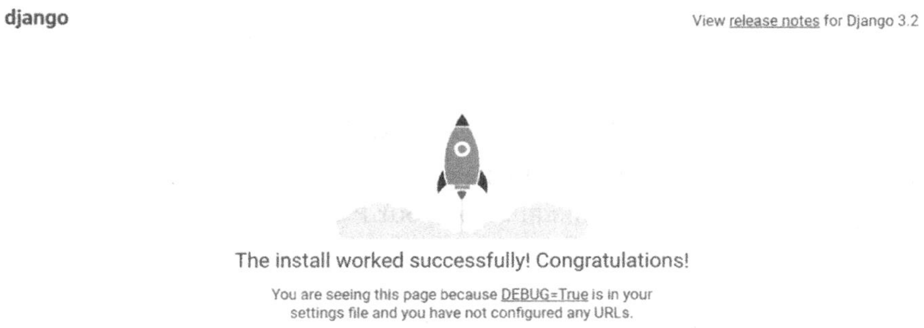
django
View release notes for Django 3.2
The install worked successfully! Congratulations!
You are seeing this page because DEBUG=True is in your settings file and you have not configured any URLs.

FIGURE 2.15 Run the server.

Performing system checks...

System check identified no issues (0 silenced).

You have 18 pending migrations. Your project might not work correctly until you will not apply the migrations for app(s): admin, auth, content types, sessions.

Run python manage.py migrate to apply them.

October 23, 2021 - 17:29:43

Django version 3.2.6, using settings 'Project.settings.'

Starting development server at http://127.0.0.1:8000/

Quit the server with CTRL-BREAK.

Note: Migrate all the models using migrate command (Figure 2.15).

Django-admin is a command line that's helps you with managing all the tasks of the project:

Django-admin startproject project_name

HOW TO CHANGE THE DEFAULT PORT?

By default, your server runs on port 8080, and you can pass in an IP address and port number separately.

- C:\Users\PC\Desktop\Python-Project\Project> python manage by runserver 8080

If you want to show your work on another computer on your network, go for this command:

- C:\Users\PC\Desktop\Python-Project\Project> python manage by runserver 0.0.0.0:8080

HOW TO CHECK THE DJANGO VERSION?

To verify that Django is installed on your PC, simply type "Pip show Django" before that PIP is installed on your PC.

Example:

C:\Users\PC>pip show Django

Name: Django

Version: 3.2.6

C:\users\PC\appdata\roaming\python\python39\site-packages

Requires: asgiref, pytz, SQL parse

Required by: Django-MySQL, djangorestframework

Or,

You can check by this way too:

C:\Users\PC>python -m django --version

3.2.6

Some references for this whole installation.
https://www.stanleyulili.com/django/how-to-install-django-on -windows/

Your first program in Django:

Move inside the second project folder and create a view file using the touch command or create a new file.

- C:\Users\PC\Projects> touch view.py

Note: view.py is case-sensitive.

Now, we will edit two files:

- view.py

- url.py

```
# editing view.py file
from django.http.response import HttpResponse
def print(request):
    return HttpResponse("Hello World!")
```

In view.py, you will write your logic here and return the result to the template.

```
from .views import *
from django.urls import path
urlpatterns = [
  path('', login,name="login"),
  path('register', register,name="register"),
]
```

In url.py, we add a path to our view with the name as above path=" register" and leave the path space empty to render the template as the main page of the project. Way to write the path:

Syntax: path('URL', view method, name)

Note: Import all the views method from view by using this line:

From .view import * (* is asterisk symbol which import everything from a particular file.)

Template File

The only way to render your content on the browser is by using templates. These are called Static files in your project. Make a different folder of that, and then add your files to it.

Don't forget to add the Static path in setting.py in the project folder. For media, CSS files, the folder will be different outside your project folder. Every application can access the folder only if your images and style sheets are applicable on all other applications.

```
<!doctype html>
<html lang="en">
 <head>
  <title>Title</title>
  <!-- Required meta tags -->
 </head>
 <body>
  {% block content %}
```

```
    {% endblock %}
 <!-- Optional JavaScript -->
 <!-- jQuery first, then Popper.js, then Bootstrap
JS -->
 </body>
 </html>
```

CREATING A PROJECT AND DEPLOYING

We can create a new project using the star project command, followed by the name of the project first (you can change it). This command will create a new folder with the given name of the project in the same directory. Now, move to the new directory using the cd command and deploy it on the local server.

After deploying, you will have a bunch of files on the command-line interface with URL in it. Copy that URL to your browser, and you will get an introductory message. Without copying, just press Ctrl + link (URL). It will automatically open your browser and deploy your project locally. Once you are done with your project, press Ctrl +c on the command line to exit from the server.

Deploying with Heroku

Heroku is the cloud hosting platform; it supports the various languages and web framework now we're on Django Python. So once your Django project is ready, you will sign up for a free Heroku account. Heroku offers at least five ways to deploy your project:

1. Git

2. Github

3. Docker

4. API

5. Web

Now sign in your Heroku account, and then enable the multi-factor authentication (MFA) to increase the protection of your account. It is also called as two-factor authentication.

- Install the Heroku CLI.

- If Heroku is already in your system, then check its version using Heroku –version.

- If not, then run the command in the terminal, run Heroku.

- To check 2fa status, Heroku auth – help.

- Now, login the Heroku CLI with Heroku login, and setup your 2fa.

- Now create the Heroku using Heroku create name_of_project.

- Heroku adds a remote server to your file, i.e., .git/config file hit enter.

- Command Heroku app will list all the apps once.

- Heroku git:remote – app name_of you_app will set the remote.

When it is created, then you will get the public web address .herokuapp .com

And your main address is like https://name_of _project. herokuapp.co m. Now you can able to see on your browser.

CHAPTER SUMMARY

This chapter covered the installation of Django and Python with simple steps. It also covered some PIP installation commands. You can also check Django's official site to learn more about fifferent types of IDEs and the first Hello World program in Django.

## CHAPTER 3

File Structure

IN THIS CHAPTER

➤ Getting to know about file structure

➤ Working with static files

➤ URL dispatcher

The previous chapter covered various IDEs for Python languages, Python, and Django installation from scratch. It also covered some PIP installation commands.

EXAMINING THE PROJECT STRUCTURE AND APPS

Django makes a directory structure to manage different parts of the web application wisely. It builds a project and an app folder for this.

Creating a proper project and organizing it helps keep the project DRY (Don't Repeat Yourself) and clean. When we create a project, Django itself makes a root directory of the project with the proper project name you have given on it. It contains the necessary files that provide basic functionalities to your web applications.

- **Application:** It (app) is a Python package that adds features to your project. You can create new apps with the startapp command "python manage.py startup myApp".

You typically enable apps by adding string in the INSTALLED_APPS list in the setting.py file:

DOI: 10.1201/9781003310495-3

```
INSTALLED_APPS = [
  'django.contrib.admin',
  'django.contrib.auth',
  'django.contrib.contenttypes',
  'django.contrib.sessions',
  'django.contrib.messages',
  'django.contrib.staticfiles',
  'myApp', #this you app
]
```

- **Project:** It is a collection of settings for an instance of Django. If you are using Django the first time, you'll have to take care of some initial setup. You will need to generate some code that organizes a Django project: a collection of settings for an instance of Django, including database configuration and many more. Use the Django-admin tool to generate a project folder.

```
├── 09-Hello-World <-- Project root
│   ├── db.sqlite3 <-- Database
│   ├── manage.py  <-- Management tool
│   ├── myapp       <-- Custom app
│   ├── forum       <-- Custom app
│   ├── myadmin     <-- Custom app
│   └── mysite      <-- Project package
└── venv <-- Virtual environment (Django + Python)
```

Handling projects in Django.

EXPLORING THE PROJECT FOLDER

The project root contains the database, manage.py file, and all the apps not installed in the environment folder. Django package and Python are installed in the venv folder.

It uses a directory structure to arrange the different parts of the web application. Now, we will discuss the Django app structure and the project structure in further detail here.

File structure.

Let's understand the function of the files that are shown in the above image. First, we will discuss the Project folder.

Manage.py

The file is used basically as a command-line utility and for deploying, debugging, or running our web application. You can read all the details of your project in manage.py. It works as a command-line utility for our projects. It is a tool for debugging, deploying, and running Django web applications also. The files consist of running the server, makemigrations or migrations, and several other commands, which we perform in the code editor. It serves the same things as Django-admin but also provides some project-specific functionality.

It contains code to run servers, makemigrations or migrations, etc.

- **runserver**: It is used to run the server for our web application, provided with the Django Framework.

- **Migration**: It applies the changes done to our models into the database.

- **makemigrations**: It applies new migrations that have been carried out due to the changes in the database.

1. **__init__.py**: It lets you know that the directory contains code; basically, this file is empty and is the only way to tell that this particular directory is a package. Its function is to tell the Python interpreter that this directory is a package and involvement of this __init.py__ files in it. If you delete this init.py file, Python will no longer look at the modules inside it and some of your files will fail. There is no need of this file on Python version 3.3 and above. All the package are considered a namespace. __init__ is the reserved in Python class name.

2. **setting.py**: This file is the master configuration file in the Django project. It holds the configuration values which need to work, information about templates, and databases. It is a core file in Django that contains all the configurations that web apps need to do. Here, you can install your app, which you will create for your project. Most of the project configuration happens in the setting .py. It contains sqlite3 as the built-in database. We can replace this database with Mysql, PostgreSQL, or MongoDB after changing a few settings in setting.py according to the web application we create.

For example, the default database configuration looks like this:

```
DATABASES = {
  'default': {
    'ENGINE': 'django.db.backends.sqlite3',
    'NAME': BASE_DIR / 'db.sqlite3',
  }
}
```

For PostgreSQL database, we would do something like this:

```
DATABASES = {
'default': {
'ENGINE': 'django.db.backends.postgresql_psycopg2',
'NAME': database_name,
'USER': 'username',
'PASSWORD': 'password',
'HOST': 'localhost',
'PORT': '',
}
}
```

For changing your time zone:

```
TIME_ZONE = 'UTC'
```

For security purposes: This enables debugging logs to be displayed when hitting error rather than HTTP status, i.e., 200, 505,400, and many more. It is good to put it True locally for error checking, but it should be false at the production level.

```
#WARNING: don not run with debug turned on in
production!
DEBUG = True
```

Middleware

In every programming language, Middleware works for processing during request and response execution. It is used to perform a function in the application. The functions can be a security session, crisp, authentication, and many more. It is hooked into Django request/response processing. It is a light low-level plugin system for entire Django's input or output.

How does this work?

When a user makes a request to server from any application, A handler WSGI get started which handles the following things:

1. Resolves the requested URL

2. Call the view function

3. Process exception methods

4. Loop through each of the response methods.

5. Loads all the Middleware's classes which written in MIDDLEWARE tuple in setting.py.

Types of Middleware

1. Built-in Middleware

2. Custom Middleware

Built-in Middleware are default present in Django when you just create your project. You can also check in setting.py portion name MIDDLEWARE.

```
MIDDLEWARE = [
  'django.middleware.security.SecurityMiddleware',
  'django.contrib.sessions.middleware.SessionMidd
leware',
  'django.middleware.common.CommonMiddleware',
  'django.middleware.csrf.CsrfViewMiddleware',
  'django.contrib.auth.middleware.AuthenticationM
iddleware',
  'django.contrib.messages.middleware.MessageMidd
leware',
  'django.middleware.clickjacking.XFrameOptionsMi
ddleware',
]
```

All these Middleware have their own functionality. Some is for security purposes, session creation, and csrf which prevent our sites from various attacks. There is also authentication Middleware used for security.

Custom Middleware

You can have your own Middleware and install your Middleware in the MIDDLEWARE portion at last.

How to Create Middleware?

1. Create Python package within a file named as middleware in __ init__.py.

2. Create a file named custommiddleware.py and use regular class and functions.

3. Now write Middleware as function or class whose object are callable.

```
class CustomMiddleware:
  def _init_(self, getback_response):
    self.gebackt_response = getback_response
  def _call_(self, request):
    # This Code that is executed in each request
before the view is called
    response = self.getback_response(request)
    # This Code that is executed in each request
after the view is called
    return response
  def process_view(request, view_func, view_args,
view_kwargs):
    # The code is executed just before the view is
called
  def process_exception(request, exception):
    # The code is executed if an exception is raised
  def process_template_response(request, response):
    # This code will execute if the response
contains a render() method
    return response
```

Also, provide various built-in Middleware that will allow you to write your Middleware. See in setting.py file of Django project that already contains multiple Middleware to maintain the application's security.

These are in-built Middleware in the file of setting.py. To activate, Middleware app in your MIDDLEWARE, it should be within a single quote like below:

```
MIDDLEWARE = [
  ' your_app_name.middleware_directory.custom_mid
dleware_file.CustomMiddleware_class,
```

```
'django.middleware.clickjacking.XFrameOptionsMi
ddleware',
]
```

Middleware Methods

1. process_view (request, view_func, view_args, view_kwargs)

   It surely takes the HttpRequest object, function object, list of an argument passed to the view. It returns either None or HttpResponce where the result shows.

2. process_template_responce (request, response)

   It takes two parameters, the first is a reference of HttpRequest, and the second is the HttpResponse object. It returns a response object that implements the render method.

3. process_exception(request, exception)

   This method takes two arguments, the first is the HttpRequest object, and the second is the Exception class object that is read by the view function.

urls.py

URL is a universal resource locator used to provide the addresses of the resources that are present there on the internet. It contains all the site deployment data, such as server names and ports, that we should have for our website. In simple words, it tells Django that a user comes with this URL, where to redirect them to the particular website or image whatever it is.

```
from django.urls import path
# from .urls import *
urlpatterns = [
  path('',include('First.urls')),
  path('',include('Framework.urls')),
  path('admin/', admin.site.urls),

]
```

URL Mapping

Now, we will learn about the routing of applications. In the introduction, we learned about MTV and that Django is a web application framework that receives user requests through URL locator and responds. To handle the URL, Django uses the URLs module. The above example shows how URLs are defined in Django.

URLs contain various functions, paths (routes, views, kwargs, names), and first arguments as a route of string or regex type. In the second argument, the view is defined, which returns a response (template) to this user.

Most Commonly Used Django URL Functions

	.	Example
path(route, view, kwargs=None, name=None)	It will return an element for inclusion in url patterns	path('index', views. index, name='main-view')
include(module, namespace = None):	It is a function that takes a full Python import path URLconf module that should be "included" in this place	

Let's create a function in the view.py, and this function will be mapped from the url.py of the same folder.

```
# this is the url.py
from Django.contrib import admin
from Django.URLs import path
from myapp import views Or (from myapp import *)
urlpatterns = [
  path('index/', index, name="index"),
]
```

Now, run the server and enter localhost:8000/index to the browser. The followed URL will be mapped into the list of URLs and call the function from the views file. This is called URL mapping.

views.py

```
from Django. shortcuts import render
from django.http import HttpResponse,
HttpResponseNotFound
from django.views.decorators.http import
require_http_methods
def index(request):
  return HttpResponse('<h1>This is Http GET request
for index page.</h1>')
```

Views are represented as Python function or a method of a Python class. But in the early time there were function-based views, as Django start growing, the Django's developer added class-based views.

Class-based views add extra feature and extensibility to Django views. It has many built-in class-based views.

Examples:

- **Base Views**

  o View

  o Template View

  o Redirect View

- **Generic Display View**

  o Details View

  o List View

- **Generic Editing View**: It will inherit from django.views.generic .CreateView.

  o FormView

  o CreateView

  o UpdateView

  o DeleteView

```
class CustomCreateView(View):
 templateName = 'form.html'
 formName = MyForm
 def get(self, request, *args, **kwargs):
  form = self.formName
  return render(request, template_name, {'form': form})
 def post(self, request, *args, **kwargs):
  form = self.formName(request.POST)
  if form.is_valid():
   form.save()
   return HttpResonseRedirect('main')
  else:
   return render(request, self.templateName,
{'form': form})
```

- **Functions-based View:** They are callable function. It inherits the method as_view() which uses a dispatch () method depending on the HTTP verb (get, post, and so on). They accept an HttpRequest object and return raise as exception.

Advantages:

1. Simple to implement.

2. Easy to read and understand it's working.

3. Direct usage of decorators.

Disadvantages:

- Hard to extend as class-based views to reuse the code.

- Handling various HTTP method using branching.

```
def index(request):
  return HttpResponse('<h1>This is Http GET request
for index page.</h1>')
```

You can go for any method. It totally depends on the context and the needs.

wsgi.py
It stands for deploying our applications onto servers like Apache etc. **WSGI (Web Server Gateway Interface)** can be a specification describing how the servers interact with web applications. Here you will not be using the webserver, but the WSGI server will take care of it. It describes the way how servers interact with the applications.

asgi.py
Asynchronous Server Gateway: It is an interface that works similar to WSGI, but this is more useful than the others because it gives better freedom in Django development.

EXPLORING THE APP FOLDER

This project folder contains all the app default directories. Let's have a look into the Django app structure in detail.

File structure.

Let's go over the files of the first app folder in the application directory to understand what they are used for.

- **_init_.py**: This file is usually an empty file that marks this directory as a Python package and has the same functionality as the _init_.py file in the Django project structure.

- **__pycache__**: This contains byte code that makes the program start faster.

- **Admin.py**: Django has an automatic admin interface in admin that you can use to manage content. admin.py is used for registering the models into the Django admin panel. All the present models have a unique superuser admin which can control the information that is being stored. Here you can register your model for use in the Admin Panel of that particular application. We will cover the model incoming chapter. We will be using the package named django-import-export for importing and exporting the data through the Django Admin.

```
from django.contrib import admin
from .models import *
# Register your models here.
admin.site.register(Register)
```

- **apps.py**: This file is a generic entry point which deals with the application configuration of the apps. This helps the user include any application configuration and you can also add some of the attribute of the application.

```
From Django. Apps import AppConfig
class FirstConfig(AppConfig):
  default_auto_field = 'django.db.models.BigAutoF
ield'
  name = 'First'
```

- **views.py**: Views are the Python function that receives the web request and returns a response. It helps us what we see when we render a Django Web application. It is very crucial, file.view.py is responsible for actually handling the HTTP requests.

  Import all URLs in your view file for further usage.

  ```
  from .models import *
  def User(request):
  return render(request,'user_details.html')
  ```

Migration Folder

The migration folder contains the migration files for the app. These are used to apply changes to the database and have a version control feature for the database schema. Whenever we hit the make migration and migrate command, changes are automatically applied.

models.py

These are the blueprints of the database structure that we are using, and hence contain the information of the database. It is the one of important files in your app. It follows the MTV design architecture.

```
from Django.DB import models
# Create your models here.
class Register(models.Model):
  Username=models.CharField(max_length=20)
```

urls.py

It handles and searches all the URLs for URL patterns. The file is to link the Views .py in the App with the host web URL apps.py. In urls.py,^ means that URL starts and $ means the end of the URL. No additional content can be added after or before it.

tests.py

This file contains different test cases for the working of the application.

This file is present in almost every application whenever you create it individually. It will help you to write the simple test cases for the database.

Files and Directories to Create
When you are working with Django project, you will create many new additional files and directories along the way. The most common files are as follows:

- **The Templates Directory**: An another important component of Django project. Templates are the 'T' of MTV pattern. You can write the display logic of your website in templates.

    It basically contains different HTML files. You can create template folder in your root directory.

- **The Static Directory**: You should create static directory in your root directory. This will contain the CSS files, JavaScript files, and images that are considered as static files.

DJANGO COMMANDS

Let's discuss some Django commands.

Create a Project's Directory Structure
The following command makes Project Directory. A project can have multiple apps in it.

- Django-admin.py startproject project_name

Create New App in Project
The following command makes App Directory. You can create multiple apps in your project.

    python manage.py startapp APPNAME

Run the Server
The following command helps run to deploy your project on a local server:

- python manage.py run server

Create Database Migration
makemigrations command creates the migration files. These files are moved with the rest of the code and applied in other environments:

- python manage.py makemigrations

Migrate the Database

migrates command updates the database schema. Always use the following command after making migrations:

- python manage.py migrate

Create Admin User

createsuperuser command creates the main administration account. This user has all permission by default (add, edit, update, delete). When we run this command in the project folder terminal, they ask for email, username, and password. Make sure that you must use a strong password and unique username.

- Python manage.py createsuperuser.

Create Admin User Git Bash

- winpty python manage.py createsuperuser

DJANGO IS A LOOSELY COUPLED FRAMEWORK

It is called a loosely coupled framework because of its *MVT pattern*, a variant of the MVC architecture that is entirely different from server code. It helps in separating the server code from the client-related code. These components support each other and they reduce the risk of maintaining the project applications. Django is called a loosely coupled framework.

Django's URL Configuration

There is some excellent example of this principle in practice. In a Django application, the URL definitions and the view functions they call are loosely coupled.

If two chunks of code are loosely coupled, the changes constantly made to one of the sections will have little or no effect on the other.

ADDITIONAL CONFIGURATION

What extra can you add to your Django project?

- Bootstrap
- Static Files

- Media Files

- Templates

These will cover all the necessary things to install Bootstrap in your project. So let's first talk about what Bootstrap is. It is the most well-liked CSS framework for developing responsive and mobile-based websites rapidly without any problem. It includes various classes which you can use in the HTML tags. It is a library of HTML, CSS, and JS that only focuses on simplifying the development of web pages. There are various ways to add Bootstrap to your project.

- **Install the Bootstrap in your local system**: Visit this official site of Bootstrap "https://getbootstrap.com/docs/3.4/getting-started" and click on the Download Bootstrap button; it will download on your PC. Then extract files from the downloaded zip folder and then you just need to copy that folder in your project and add it. You will also get three options before downloading it: Bootstrap itself, Source code, and Sass.

- **Directly add its CDN in your project in script tags**: Below that, on the same official site, you will get Bootstrap CDN. Copy that CDN links and paste them into your HTML file. Paste the CSS link in the head section of HTML and script links in the script tag itself above the </body> body closing tag.

Example:

```
#this is CSS Link
  <link rel="stylesheet" href="https://stackpath
.bootstrapcdn.com/bootstrap/4.3.1/css/bootstrap.min
.css">
#this is Js link
  <script src="https://stackpath.bootstrapcdn.com/
bootstrap/4.3.1/js/bootstrap.min.js"></script>
```

- Using the terminal, run the command to install it.

    1. Install with bower, with simple command as given below:

        C:\Users\PC\Project> bower install bootstrap

2. Install with npm

C:\Users\PC\Project> npm install bootstrap@3

3. Install with composer

C:\Users\PC\Project> composer require twbs/bootstrap

But in Django, you can use a terminal that makes things easier to implement. Now make a folder or directory in your project named static, and then add some lines of code in your setting.py, which is in your main project folder.

```
import os
STATIC_DIR = os.path.join(BASE_DIR, 'static')
STATIC_URL = '/static/'
```

To load your static files in the template, add the below code in your base .html in the beginning and then you can get access to your static folder.

```
{% load static %}
```

Add the above lines of code in setting.py. Make sure your directory will be the same as mentioned. The above code defines that you import the os module and then join the application's base path with your static folder. Now load this static folder in your project base template, i.e., the standard template file which contains the same rendering content on every page of your project. Adding media files in your project is the same as above; you just need to change the name of the templates folder as media and then add online in your setting.py

```
STATICFILES_DIRS = [
  STATIC_DIR, MEDIA_DIR
]
```

Perform the steps one by one. Don't mix them. Try them one at a time. The above code defines that you add both paths.

- **Template:** Django takes the help of HTML to render its content on the browser. You need to have only a templates folder in your project. Then add the path of the template in setting.py as below:

```
# setting.py
TEMPLATES = [
  {
    'BACKEND': 'django.template.backends.django.Dj
angoTemplates',
    'DIRS': ['template'], #write your folder name in
[].
    'APP_DIRS': True,
    'OPTIONS': {
      'context_processors': [
        'django.template.context_processors.debug',
        'django.template.context_processors.request',
        'django.contrib.auth.context_processors.a
uth',
        'django.contrib.messages.context_processo
rs.messages',
      ],
    },
  },
]
```

Django Static (CSS, JavaScript, image) Configuration.

- **Loading Images Example**

```
<!DOCTYPE html>
<html lang="en">
<head>
  <meta charset="UTF-8">
  <title>Index Page</title>
    {% load static %}
</head>
<body>
<img src="{% static '/wallpaper.jpeg' %}" alt="My
image" height="300px" width="700px"/>
</body>
</html>
```

- **Loading JavaScript**

```
<!DOCTYPE html>
#index.html
<html lang="en">
<head>
  <meta charset="UTF-8">
  <title>Index</title>
    {% load static %}
  <script src="{% static '/js/script.js' %}"
type="text/javascript"></script>
</head>
<body>
</body>
</html>
```

- **Script.js**

```
alert("I am Learning Python with Django");
```

<script src="{% static '/js/script.js' %}" type="text/javascript"></script>.
This link is used to link external javaScript file to index.html.

- **Django Loading CSS**

```
{% load static %}
<!DOCTYPE html>
<html lang="en">
<head>
  <meta charset="UTF-8">
  <title>Index Page</title>
  <link href="{% static 'css/style.css' %}"
rel="stylesheet">
</head>
<body>
<p> I am Learning Python with Django </p>
</body>
</html>
```

  style.css

```
p{
color : yellow;
}
```

URL Dispatcher

Django allows you to design URLs clean and usable. To create URLs for an app, you create a Python module informally called URLconf, i.e., URL configuration.

How does Django process a request?

It determines the root URLconf module to use. The value will be the ROOT_URLCONF setting, but if the incoming HTTPRequest object has URL conf attribute (), the discount will be used in the place of the ROOT_URLCONF setting.

It loads the Python module and paths for the variable urlpatterns.

It runs through each URL_pattern. This should be a sequence of Django .URLs.path().

It imports the given view once the URL pattern matches. The view gets past the following arguments.

1. An instance of HttpRequest.

2. If the matched URL pattern contained no name groups, then it matches from the regular expression.

3. The keyword is made up of any name parts matched by the path expression that is provided, overridden with arguments specified in the optional kwargs.

    If no URL matches, or if an exception is raised during any point in this process, Django invokes an error handling.

Example:

```
from Django. URLs import path
from. import views
urlpatterns = [
  path('student/id/,student,name=student_login),
  path('student/<int:year>/',
student,name=student_login),
 path('student/<int:year>/<int:month>/', views.
month_archive),
]
```

Note: To get a value from the URL, use angle brackets < >.

<int: name>, this will add data type for URL so that user can pass only one integer.

Note: No need to add a leading slash / with any URL because every URL has that. Once the URL request is passed, that URL should give a similar path which you provide in url.py. Otherwise, it will raise an error.

Modules vs. package – so first, what is modules in Django?

Both sometimes make others a bit confused as what is module and packages. So let's take a moment to explain them.

- **Package:** It is refers to a collection of Python module. It is a single Python file, where a package is a collection of files. It contains an additional file named __init__.py to make difference between such modules. There are so many packages in Python that you can import them into your Django modules.

  o abc

  o datetime

  o http

  o json

  o math

  o random

  o importlib

  o functools

  o collections

  o os

  o multiprocessing

  o inspect

  o pdb

CHAPTER SUMMARY

In this chapter, we have learned how Django projects are structured, how each component works with other files, and to create a web application. We also discussed Django app's extra features with some examples.

## CHAPTER 4

Django's Model

IN THIS CHAPTER

➢ Getting to know the working of model

➢ Python built-in function

➢ Database configuration

In the previous chapter, we have learned about file structure in Django. The chapter explained built-in files like model.py, view.py, etc..

In addition to the structure of Django files, an explanation of each file in the application and the main project was also provided.

The topic we will discuss in this chapter is a critical one: how can you play with your data structure in Django?

FUNDAMENTALS OF DJANGO'S MODEL

This chapter covers:

1. Definition of model

2. Installing the model

3. How to create and use model

4. Different types of fields in model

5. Model formats

DOI: 10.1201/9781003310495-4

In Django, a model is the source of information about your data. It consists of the essential fields and behaviors of the data which you have stored in the database. Every model maps to a single table of databases.

Example:

```
from Django.DB import models
class Event(models.Model):
  name = models.CharField('Event Name',
max_length=120)
  event_date = models.DateTimeField('Event Date')
  venue = models.CharField(max_length=120)
  manager = models.ForeignKey(max_length=60)
  description = models.TextField(blank=True,
default= None)
```

In the above example, we have event class, and it has various fields like its name, event_data, venue, manager, and description.

The project field defines one foreign essential type: manager. The project field that defines the relationship with the Event model has two additional attributes:

1. **Null**: This decides whether the element can be defined as null. The fact that this attribute is in the project field means that its tasks are not necessarily related to a project.

2. **Default**: This sets the default value that the field will have.

To use this model, we need to register it in admin.py so that we can get all the data in our model (event).

```
from Django. contrib import admin
from .models import *
# Register your models here.
admin.site.register(Event)
```

It represents a subclass of (django.db.models.Model) and each field represents database field (column).

We have written the code; now let's create the table for database. The first step is to activate this model in Django project. Edit the setting.py file again and look at the INSTALLED_APP setting. Basically, INSTALLED_APPS tells Django which apps are activated for a given project. By default, it looks something like this:

```
INSTALLED_APPS = [
  'django.contrib.admin',
  'django.contrib.auth',
  'django.contrib.contenttypes',
  'django.contrib.sessions',
  'django.contrib.messages',
  'django.contrib.staticfiles',
  'NewApp',
]
```

'NewApp' refers to the book's app we are working on. Each INSTAL LED_APPS is represented by its full Python path – the path of packages, separated by dots, leading to its app package. Example: Django.contrib. sites.

Now the Django app has been activated in the setting.py, we can thus create the database table in our database. First, let's validate the model by running the following command:

- python manage.py validate

The validate command checks whether your model's syntax and logic are correct. You will see the message zero is no error found. Any time you think of your problem with models, run python manage.py validate in the terminal. It catches all the standard model problems.

How to create a model

```
from Django.db import models
from django.contrib.auth.models import User
class Post(models.Model):
    title = models.CharField(max_length=20)
    description = models.CharField(max_length=100)
```

This is what your model looks like; let's discuss every point of the code.

First, you will have to write an import model from Django. db to model it in our code. The second line shows that we import a built-in user from Django.contrib.auth.models. This user is available in our Administration Panel. We have an entire chapter on the Admin Panel of Django.

Every model name should begin with a capital letter and the remaining letters should be in lowercase. In the above code, we have to make a POST model, and its first letter is a capital, and the rest are lowercase. It should be written in class syntax:

- Class ModelName():

    // rest of the code.

model.Models is the parameter used to pass in class because thereafter we get access to use models in our field, which we are going to add for storing different values in the database.

The title and description fields are specified as the class attribute, and each attribute maps to a database column.

```
CREATE TABLE POST (
  "id" INT NOT NULL PRIMARY KEY, //automatically
allot
  "title" varchar(20) NOT NULL,
  "description" varchar(100) NOT NULL
);
```

The id field is autocreated. The name of the table is similar to the name of the model. This is the way to store your data in the database of the model.

Title and description – Implies having varchar data type in the language of SQL queries.

Once your model has been defined, you need to tell Django that you will use that model in your project. First, you will have to add your application name in INSTALLED_APPS in the setting.py:

```
INSTALLED_APPS = [
  #...
  'new app,
  #...
]
```

Then run the migrate command, i.e., python manage.py make migrations, and then run the command python manage.py migrate to update your database.

Different Types of Fields

Fields are the suitable data type for your data. It is defined inside the model class.

```
from django.db import models
from django.contrib.auth.models import User
```

```
class Post(models.Model):
    title = models.CharField(max_length=20)
    age = models.IntegerField(max_length=100)
 date = models.DateField()
 marks = models.IntegerField()
```

Here the fields are CharField and IntegerField. There are various data types in Django. Let's have a look at it:

Field Name	Class	Description
AutoField	BigAutoField(options)	It is an IntegerField that automatically increments
BigAutoField	BigAutoField(options)	It is a 64-bit integer, ranging from 1 to 9223372036854775807
BigIntegerField	BigIntegerField(options)	It is a 64-bit integer, ranging from 9223372036854775808 to 9223372036854775807
BinaryField	BinaryField(options)	It is a field to store raw binary data
BooleanField	BooleanField(options)	
CharField	DateField(auto=False, auto_now_add=False, options)	It is a type used to define that your text is represented as a character
DecimalField	DecimalField(max_digits='', decimal_places='', other)	It is a fixed precision decimal number, represented in Python language by a decimal instance
DurationField	DurationField(options)	It is a field for storing periods of time
EmailField	EmailField(max_length=254, options)	It checks that the value is a valid email address
FileField	FileField(upload_to=path, max_length=100, options)	It is a file-upload field
DateTimeField	DateTimeField(auto=False, auto_now_add=False, options)	It is represented in Python by a datetime.date instance. It is also used for data and time by a DateTime.DateTime instance
FloatField	FloatField(options)	It is a floating-point number by a float instance

(Continued)

Field Name	Class	Description
ImageField	ImageField(upload_to=path, height_field=None, width_field=None, max_length=100, **options)	It gets all attributes and methods from FileField and also validates that the uploaded object is a valid image
IntegerField	IntegerField(**options)	It is an integer field, and its range is from2147483648 to 2147483647, which is safe in all databases supported by Django
NullBooleanField	NullBooleanField(options)	Like a BooleanField, it allows NULL as one of the options
PositiveIntegerField	PositiveIntegerField(extra_options)	It must be either positive or zero (0). Its range from 0 to 2147483647 is safe in all databases supported by Django
SmallIntegerField	SmallIntegerField(extra_options)	It is like an IntegerField only, allowing values under a certain (database-dependent) point
TextField	TextField(options)	The form widget for this field is a Textarea access large data text
TimeField	TimeField(auto=False, auto_now_add=False, options)	A time represented in Python by a datetime.time instance

HOW DO DJANGO MODELS WORK?

Django's models provide an OBM (object-relational mapping) to the underlying database. It is a powerful programming technique that makes working with bulk data and relational databases much more straightforward.

SQL is challenging to learn, but the technique makes everything simple and provides the mapping to an object (the O in ORM) (Figure 4.1).

What Is Fields Option?

Each field (attributes) requires some arguments that are used to set attributes value. For example, max_length, Null, blank, etc. have many more options.

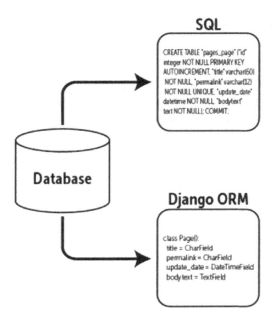

FIGURE 4.1 Django models.

Field Options

Options	Description
Null	: empty store values as NULL in the database
Blank	: used to allow the field to be blank
Choices	It is an iterable (a list or tuple) of two tuples to use as choices for any field
Default	The default value for the field can be a value or a callable object

Explanation

Here you get a quick summary of the most oft-used options in the Django model. Each field takes a set of area: few to take only one, but others take more than one. For example, CharField takes max_length, which specifies the size of the VARCHAR to store the data in the dataset and Null attributes.

- **Null:** If Null is defined as True, Django will store empty values in the database. But the default is false.

- **Blank**: If this option is True, the field is allowed to be blank. Default is False. If a domain has blank =False, the field will be required. In True, an empty value will pass.

- **Choices**: An iterable (e.g., a list of tuples) of 2-tuple are used in this field. The default form widget, i.e., your form structure, will select a box instead of the standard text field.

```
marks = (
  ("60", "10"),
  ("50", "50"),
  ("70", "30"),
  ("60", "40"),
  )
class StudentData(models.Model):
  semester = models.CharField(
   max_length = 20,
   choices = marks,
   )
```

- **Default**: The default value for the field. It can be a value or callable object. Every time a different object is created.

- **Help_text**: This will "help" text to be displayed with the form widget.

Different types of keys:

- **Primary key**: A primary key to ensure data in the specific column is unique. The field is the primary key for the model if true.

  If you don't specify primary = True for any fields in your model, Django will automatically add an IntergerField to hold the primary key. This file is read=only. If you change the value of this primary key on an existing object and then save it, a new entity will be created along with the old one. For example,

```
from Django.DB import models
class Student(models.Model):
  name = models.CharField(max_length=100,
primary_key=True)
```

How to store data in the Student model with the object.create() is given below.

```
Student_name = Student.objects.create(name='Rohan')
Student_name.name = 'john'
Student_name.save()
Student_name.objects.values_list('name')
```

- **Foreign key**: It accepts another argument that defines the details of how the relation works.

  When an object referenced by the Foreign Key is deleted, Django will copy the behavior of the SQL constraint by the on_delete argument. For example, if you have a nullable Foreign Key, then your referenced object is as follows:

```
user = models.ForeignKey(
  User,
  On_delete=models.CASCADE,
  blank=True,
  null=True,
)
```

- **CASCADE**: Cascade delete. Django follows the behavior of the SQL constraint ONE DELETE CASCADE and deletes the object containing the foreign key, where the user is imported from the Django itself.

- **Basic Data Access**: Once you have created a model, Django automatically provides a high-level Python API for working with those models. Suppose we have one model name 'Student' in model.py. Let's try out to get data from this Student model in the terminal. Make sure your model files should have all these attributes.

  o >>> From model import *

  o >>> S1 = Student(name='Komal', address='ABC, XYZ Avenue ,'city='NY', country='UK')

  o >>> S1.save()

  o >>> S2 = Student(name='Arsh', address='EFG,Z Avenue ,'city='NJ', country='USA')

  o >>> Student_list = Student.objects.all()

o >>> Student_list

o [<Student :Student object>,<Student: Student object>].

The following few lines will help you to make understand the code clearly:

- First, import the Student model class. This lets you interact with the database table that contains students.

- Create the object for the model student with values for each field: name, address, city, country.

- To save this object into the database, call the inbuilt save() method.

- To retrieve object, use the attribute Student.objects.all(). Behind the scenes, Django executes an SQL SELECT statement here.

Adding Model String

When we printed out the list of students, all we got was the output and it is difficult to read deatails from it.

- [<Student: Student object>, <Student :Student objects>]

We can fix this by adding __unicode__() to our Student class. A __unicode__() method tells Python to display the 'Unicode' of an object.

What Is Unicode Object?

If you define __unicode__() method with any model, Django will call it when it needs to render an object in a context (as String).

```
class Student(models.Model):
    name = models.CharField(max_length=30)
    address = models.CharField(max_length=50)
    city = models.CharField(max_length=60)
        def __unicode__(self):
        return self.name, self.address, self.city
#OUTPUT
<Student:'Komal'>, <Student:'ABC, XYZ Avenue' >
<Student:'NY' >,<Student:'UK' >]
```

Magic method or Dunder Method

Use the pattern below to handle your magic method:

__str__ () and __unicode_() methods : In Python 2, the object model specifies __str__( ) and __unicode__() methods. If these methods exist in your model code, they must return str (bytes) and unicode (text),

respectively. Here the print statement and in-built method __str__()
represented a human-readable text. The methods __str__() and __uni-
code__() work on Python 2 and 3. You must define a __str__() method
returning text and apply the python_2_unicode_compatible() decorator
in python2.

```
from django.utils.encoding import
python_2_unicode_compatible
@python_2_unicode_compatible
class MyClass(object):
  def __str__(self):
    return "Instance of my class"
```

But in Python 3, @decorator is optional. Finally, note that __repr__()
must return str on all versions of Python.

- **Init**: This is the method you must have already used in your classes.
  This init is used to create an instance of the class and also works as
  a constructor.

```
class Number:
    def __init__(self, number):
        self.number = number
    def get_number(self):
      return self.number
n = Number(3)
print(n.get_number())
#OUTPUT
3
```

  o **Iterators**: The Python iterator object must implement two unique
    methods, __iter__() and __next__(), collectively called iterator
    protocol.

    – **__iter__()**: This function returns an iterator object that goes
      through each element of the object. The following method
      can be accessed by the __next__() function.

    – **__next__()**: This function helps to get the value of next
      object. It is always used after the __iter__() method.

Example:

```
class MyIterator(six.Iterator):
  def __iter__(self):
```

```
    return self      # implement some logic here
def __next__(self):
    raise StopIteration  # implement some logic here
```

- __getitem__ and __setitem__: There are two getter and setter methods implemented by __getitem__() and __setitem__(). These methods are used in indexed attributes like arrays, dictionaries, lists, etc.

```
#way to set the value.
def __setitem__(self,name,student):
  if name in self.student:
    self.student[name] = student
  else:
    raise Exception("Student Name doesn't exist")
#way to get the value.
def __getitem__(self,name,student):
  if name in self.student:
    self.student[name] = student
  else:
    raise Exception("Student Name doesn't exist")
#way to delete the value.
def __delitem__(self,name,student):
  if name in self.student:
    del self.student[name]
    self.names.remove(name)
  else:
    raise Exception("Student Name doesn't exist")
```

__len__(): The lens method for class returns the number of students. This method would return only integer values.

```
def __len__(self):
  return len(self.names)
print(len(p))
```

- __contains__(): This method is used when using the in operator. The return value is Boolean.

Example:

```
def __contains__(self,name):
  if name in self.students:
```

```
    return True
  else:
    return False
```

- **Boolean evaluation**

  1. **__bool__**: Each and everyone has a Boolean value, which can be either True or False. The Boolean (object) returns the Boolean value of the thing. It produces a Boolean value by calling the __bool__() method.

  2. **__nonzero__**: Python 2 used the __nonzero__ method to convert an object to Boolean.

Example:

```
class MyBoolean(object):
  def __bool__(self):
    return True       # implement some logic here
  def __nonzero__(self):   # Python 2 compatibility
    return type(self).__bool__(self)
```

- Division

```
class MyDivisible(object):
  def __truediv__(self, other):
    return self / other   # implement some logic here
  def __div__(self, other):  # Python 2
compatibility
    return type(self).__truediv__(self, other)
  def __itruediv__(self, other):
    return self // other # implement some logic here
  def __idiv__(self, other): # Python 2
compatibility
    return type(self).__itruediv__(self, other)
```

Some more dunder methods

- **add**: This method involves using the + operator. We can define a custom add the method for our class.

  o a1 + a2 is equal to a1.__add__(a2)

```
def __add__(self,a2):
  a = self.
a + a2.a
  b = self.b + a2.b
  return point(x,y)
```

- **iadd**: The iadd method is like the add method. It is invoked when using the += operator.

```
def __iadd__(self,p2):
  self.x += p2.x
  self.y += p2.y
  return self
```

The method above just updates the coordinates at an instance by adding the coordinates of p2. Make sure you are returning yourself. Otherwise, it will return None and would not work as expected.

```
p1 += p2
print(p1)
```

The above method invokes the add method.
Some other useful operators

- __sub__(self,p2) (-)

- __isub__(self,p2) (-=)

- __mul__(self,p2) (*)

- __imul__(self,p2) (*=)

- __truediv__(self,p2) (\ )

- __itruediv__(self,p2) (\=)

- __floordiv__(self,p2) (\\ )

- __ifloordiv__(self,p2) (\=)

```
student_1 = 4
student_2 = 2
# Binary Operators
print (student_1.__add__(student_2))
```

```
print(student_1.__sub__(student_2))
print(student_1.__mul__(student_2))
print(student_1.__truediv__(student_2))
print(student_1.__floordiv__(student_2))
print(student_1.__pow__(student_2))
print(student_1.__mul__(student_2))
print(student_1.__lshift__(student_2))
print(student_1.__rshift__(student_2))
print(student_1.__and__(student_2))
print(student_1.__or__(student_2))
import operator
# Extended Assigments
print(operator.__iadd__(student_1,10))
print(operator.__isub__(student_1,10))
print(operator.__itruediv__(student_1,10))
print(operator.__ifloordiv__(student_1,10))
print(operator.__ipow__(student_1,10))
print(operator.__imul__(student_1,10))
print(operator.__ilshift__(student_1,10))
print(operator.__irshift__(student_1,10))
print(operator.__iand__(student_1,10))
print(operator.__ior__(student_1,10))
print(operator.__imod__(student_1,10))
# Unary Operators
print(operator.__neg__(10))
print(operator.__pos__(-680))
```

RELATIONSHIPS AND QUERY SET

Relationships

A relationship works between two relational database tables when one table has the foreign key of the other table as a primary key. It allows us to split and store data in different tables:

1. Many-to-many relationships

2. Many-to-one relationships

3. One-to-one relationships

Many-to-Many Relationships

A many-to-many relationship refers to a relationship between tables in a database. A parent row in one table contains several child rows in the second table and vice versa (in RDBMS). Use ManyToManyField to define the many-to-many relationships with the class model.

```
class Student(models.Model):
    name = models.CharField(max_length=30)
class Marks(models.Model):
  marks = models.CharField(max_length=100)
  student_model = models.ManyToManyField(Student)
```

Create a new Student:

```
add = Student.objects.create(username = 'rahul20',
first_name = 'Rahul', last_name = 'Shakya', mobile =
'77777', email = 'rahul@gmail.com')
```

Save data in the student model:

```
s1 = Student(name='Sam')
s1 = Student(name='jam')
s1.save()
```

This is how you can save student in Django. Save() is an inbuilt method which saves data in the database.

Get all the data:

```
#using all() method
data = Student.object.all()
#output
<QuerySet [ <Student:Sam>,<Student:Jam>] >
```

Retrieving Single Object from QuerySets

The get() returns the single object directly with the parameter passed in the parentheses. It finds the match object and returns it in QuerySet result.

```
# using the get() method.
get_data = Student.objects.get(pk = 1)
get_data
<Student: Jam>          ,
get_data = Student.objects.get(name = 'Jam')
get_data
[ <Student: Jam> ]
```

Filtering the Records

The QuerySet return by all() describes all records in the database. But sometimes we want to select only limited information from the database, which can be done by adding the filter conditions.

```
data_filter = Student.objects.filter(name="Sam")
```

Using exclude() Method

It returns a new QuerySet that does not match with the given parameter.

```
data_filter = Student.objects.exclude('name="Sam')
#OUTPUT
[ <Student: Jam> ]
```

Ordering Data

As you play around with the previous example, you might discover that they are being returned in seemingly random order. Sometimes you want the result in order like alphabets, series of numbers, etc., we use the order_by() method.

```
# Ascending order
ModelName.objects.all().filter(client=id).order_b
y('number')
# Descending order
ModelName.objects.all().filter(client=id).order_b
y('-number')
# Earliest
ModelName.objects.all().filter(client=id).earlies
t('number')
# Latest
ModelName.objects.all().filter(client=id).latest(
'-number')
```

first(), last(), delete(), update()

```
ModelName.objects.all().order_by('title','data').
first()
ModelName.objects.all().order_by('title','data').
last()
ModelName.objects.all().filter(id=2).delete()
ModelName.objects.all().filter(pk=id).last()
```

Chaining Lookups

You have already seen how you can filter and have also seen order_by. You can use both in a single line of code.

```
Student.objects.filter(country="US").order_by("-n
ame")
[<Studentent: 'SAM'>, <Marks: 89>]
```

Slicing Data

Suppose you have the data of thousands of Students in your database, and you want data in various forms like first Student's data, only 100 students' data, data of students between 1 and 50. The slicing concept appears. You can get data with indexing,i.e.[].

```
Student.objects.order_by('name')[0] #for only first
Student.objects.order_by('name')[0:100] # 1 to 100
excluding 100.
```

Using an operator in Django ORM:

1. And

2. Or

An operator is used to bind the condition with each other when we need the record matching with two or more requirements.

It can be done with three ways:

1. query_1 & query_2

2. filter(<condition_1> , <condtion_2>)

3. filter(<condition_1> & <condtion_2>)

Syntax

```
Student.objects.filter(name__startswith = 'Sam') &
Student.objects.filter(name__startswith = 'Jam')
Student.objects.filter( name__startswith='Sam',
name__startswith='Jam' )
 Student.objects.filter(Q(name__startswith='Sam') &
Q(name__startswith='Jam') )
```

All queries will have the same result.

How to clear Relation set:

```
p2.student.clear()
p2.student.all()
#OUTPUT
<QuerySet []>
```

Many-to-One Relationships

A many-to-one relationship is where one entity (typically a column or a set of columns) contains values that refer to another entity (a column or a group of columns) with unique values (in RDBMS).

To define many-to-one relationship, use Foreign Key:

```
from Django.DB import models
class Student(models.Model):
  first_name = models.CharField(max_length=30)
  last_name = models.CharField(max_length=30)
  def __str__(self):
    return self.first_name
class Article(models.Model):
  marks = models.CharField(max_length=100)
  student = models.ForeignKey(Student, on_
delete=models.CASCADE)
  def __str__(self):
    return self.marks
```

Examples are similar to many-to-many relationships.

Create a new Student:

```
add = Student.objects.create(username = 'rahul20',
first_name = 'Rahul', last_name = 'Shakya')
```

Save data in the student model:

```
s1 = Student(name='ROHAN')
s1 = Student(name='SOHAN')
s1.save()
```

This is how you can save student in Django. Save() is an inbuilt method which saves data in the database.

Get all the data:

```
#using all() method
data = Student.object.all()
#output
<QuerySet [<Student:ROHAN>,<Student:SOHAN>]>
```

Retrieving single object from QuerySets:
The get() returns the single object directly with the parameter passed in the parentheses. It finds the match object and returns it in QuerySet result.

```
# using the get() method.
get_data = Student.objects.get(pk = 1)
get_data
<Student: Jam>
get_data = Student.objects.get(name = 'ROHAN)
get_data
<Student: ROHAN>
```

Filtering the records:
The QuerySet return by all() describes all records in the database. But sometimes we want to select only limited information from the database, which can be done by adding the filter conditions.

```
data_filter = Student.objects.filter(name="SOHAN")
```

Using Exclude() Method:
It returns a new QuerySet contain that do not match with the given parameter.

```
data_filter = Student.objects.exclude('name="SOHAN)
#OUTPUT
<Student: SOHAN>
```

SOME IMPORTANT FIELD LOOKUPS

In Django, we have various field loops, which are similar to the SQL WHERE clause. They are only used with filter(), exclude(), and get(). Every lookup should be prefixed __name_of_lookup. It is case-sensitive.

Example:

Use of starts with the standard:

```
Student.objects.filter(fname__startswith = 'Aman')
```

Use of exact:

```
Student.objects.get(lname__exact = 'Singh')
```

Use of contains:

```
Student.objects.filter(surname__contains = 'Gill')
```

One-to-One Relationships

A one-to-one relationship exists when each row in one table has only one corresponding row in a second table.

To define a one-to-one relationship, use OneToOneField:

```
From Django.DB import models
class Student(models.Model):
  first_name = models.CharField(max_length=30)
  last_name = models.CharField(max_length=30)
  def __str__(self):
    return self.first_name
class Article(models.Model):
  marks = models.CharField(max_length=100)
  student = models. OneToOneField (Student, on_
delete=models.CASCADE)
  def __str__(self):
    return self.marks
```

Examples are similar to many-to-many relationships.
Some rules for the field:

1. A field name cannot be a Python identifier or reserved word because it will show you the Syntax error.

```
class Example(models.Model):
  break = models.IntegerField() # 'break' is a
reserved key word!
```

2. A field name should only have one underscore, not more than one underscore (__) in a row, and the field name cannot end with an underscore, and it is invalid:

```
class Example(models.Model):
  first__name = models.CharField() # 'first__name'
is a reserved word!
```

3. **Meta Options**: Model Meta is the inner class of your model class. Model Meta is used for changing your model fields' behavior like changing order options, verbose_name, and many other options. It is completely optional to add a Meta class to your model.

```
class student(models.Model):
  class Meta:
    options........
```

4. **Model Attributes**

   • **Objects**: The most crucial attribute of the model is the model's manager. It is the interface through which database query operations are provided to the Django model and is used to get the instances from the database.

   • **Model methods**:

     __str__ (): This is a "magic method" that returns a string representation of any object.

```
class Example(models.Model):
  first__name = models.CharField() # 'first__name'
is a reserved word!
```

Python model has various advantages:

• **Simplicity**: Python is not only easier than writing SQL, but it is also easier for programs to build web applications with clean, readable, and maintainable code by taking advantage of syntax.

• **Consistency**: SQL is inconsistent across different databases. A model can describe your data once, and there is no need to create different sets of SQL statements for every database to which the application will be easily deployed.

- **Version Control**: Storing models in your database makes it easier to keep track of design changes.

- **Metadata**: Having a model described in code rather than SQL allows for particular data types and provides the capacity to store much more metadata than SQL.

WHY DO WE USE MODELS?

Django's model is written in Python and provides a mapping to the underlying database structure. Django uses a model to execute SQL behind the scenes to return Python data structures – which Django calls QuerySets.

CONFIGURING THE DATABASE

We will assume you have set up a database server, activated it, and created a database within it (e.g., using CREATE DATABASE statement). If you are using SQLite, no such setup is required because SQLite uses stand-alone files in the Django file system to store its data.

SQL Lite:

```
DATABASES = {
  'default': {
    'ENGINE': 'django.db.backends.sqlite3',
    'NAME': BASE_DIR / 'db.sqlite3',
  }
}
```

In the previous chapter, we heard about setting.py. SQLite is previously added as default.

Types of Database

Setting	Database
PostgreSQL	PostgreSQL
Postgresql_psycogy2	PostgreSQL
oracle	Oracle
MySQL	MYSQL
sqlite3	SQLite

Connecting to Database

Connecting settings are used in this order:

1. Options

2. NAME, USER, PASSWORD, HOST, PORT

3. MySQL options files.

On the other hand, if you set the name of the database in OPTIONS, this will take precedence over NAME, which would override anything in an MYSQL option file.

MYSQL database:

```
# settings.py
DATABASES = {
  'default': {
    'DATABASE_ENGINE': 'django.db.backends.mysql',
    ''DATABASE_NAME': 'home/db/djangodatabase',
    ''DATABASE_USER': 'dbadmin',
    ''DATABASE_PASSWORD': '12345',
    ''DATABASE_HOST': 'localhost',
    ''DATABASE_PORT': '3306',
  }
}
```

You will need to download and install the appropriate database adapter, no matter whichever database back-end you may be using. Each one is available for free on the Web. If you have a Linux system, your distribution's package-management system might offer convenient packages (look for the package called python-PostgreSQL or python-psycopg). For example:

- DATABASE_ENGINE = "Django.DB.backends.MySQL"

- DATABASE_NAME tells Django the name of your database. For example,

- DATABASE_NAME = "djangodatabase"

If you are using SQLite, specify the full filesystem path to the database file on your filesystem.

- DATABASE_NAME = 'djangodatabase'

We are now putting the database path in the directory, like we are using "home/DB/Django database".

- DATABASE_USER tells Django which username to use when connecting to your database. If you are using SQLite, leave this blank.

- DATABASE_PASSWORD tells Django which pass to use when the database is appropriately connected to get all the stored information. If SQLite, leave this blank.

- DATABASE_HOST tells Django who the host is if your database is on the same computer as your Django installation (i.e., localhost). If SQLite, leave this blank.

Modelformsets

It is a layer of abstraction to work with the multiple forms of the same pages like

```
FormSet = modelformset_factory(User_Model, fields
=['title', 'description'], extra = 3)
```

The extra keyword argument makes multiple copies of the same form.

THE ADMIN MODULE

The administration module is convenient and is included by default with Django. It is a module that will maintain the content of the database without any difficulty. It cannot support the structure of the database because this is not the database manager. It manages the relationships between models. It contains Django permissions. You can set permissions for users according to models and CRUD operations. It is quickly established.

Installing the Admin Module

To implement the administration module, go to setting.py and edit them. In the INSTALLED_APPS setting, you need to add the new line in it:

```
# add this to INSTALLED_APPS
'django.contrib.admin'
```

CHAPTER SUMMARY

Having read this chapter, you have enough knowledge of Django models to write basic database applications. It provided some information on more advanced usage of Django's database layer. Once you've defined your models, the next step is to populate your database with data. The next chapter covers Django's Views interface.

## CHAPTER 5

Django's View

IN THIS CHAPTER

➢ Getting to know about view in Django

➢ URL routing

➢ Regular expression

In the previous chapter, we have learned about Django models and their basic database applications, types of databases in Django, and some information on more advanced usage of Django's database layers. Various types of keys and their relationships were also covered. This chapter covers Django's view interface.

In this chapter, you will learn about views, the basics and the advanced creating dynamic and static URLs for web pages: regex, class-based generic and function-based generic views, and their types.

VIEWS IN DJANGO

In Python, a view function, or view for short, is used to take a web request and returns a web response. This is accomplished by the use of HTML content on a web page, text rendering, documents, graphics, style, and other techniques. It itself contains whatever logic is necessary to return that response back to the client. This code can live anywhere on the browser you want, as long as it is on your Python path.

CONFIGURATION OF THE URLS

Whenever you start your development server, you would notice on your screen Django's welcome page. In Django, for having a new view, you will have to tell Django that index view should be displayed when someone navigates to the site root URL (name of the page). We do this by adding the new URLs.

In Django, the path() function is also used to configure URLs for mapping the view with URL. The path function is contained under the Django. url within the Django project codebase in its basic form, the path() function.

Syntax:

```
path(route, view)
```

An example of the basic path() function will be path('mypage/', views .myview)

1. The path() function can also take one optional name argument, and zero or more keyword arguments passed as a Python dictionary (a concept in Python). We will get to these details later in this book.

2. The path() function statements live in a special file called urls.py.

   When startproject created our website, it created an urls.py file in our site folder (\mysite\urls.py).

Code of simple view:

```
from Django.http import HttpResponse
def index(request):
return HttpResponse("Hello Python")
```

Let's step within this code one line at a time:
First, you import the class HttpResponse, which lives in Django.HTTP module. Import this for later use in code.

- Next, you define a function called index – the view function.

- Each view function takes at least one parameter, which is simply called request by convention. This object contains information about the current Web request that has triggered this view and it's an instance of the class: Django.HTTP.HttpRequest.

- The name of the view function does not matter whatever it is; it doesn't have to be named.

- In a certain way, Django has to recognize it. So every URL should have a unique name so that no confusion may arises. We called it index so that it could render the index page.

- The function is a simple one line that merely returns an HttpResponse object that has been instantiated with the text "Hello Python".

This code is for implementing the basics of views in Django; the above code tells what to import to use the URL in the project.

MAPPING URLS TO VIEWS

This diagram may be as short or as long as you need it to be. It has the ability to refer to other mappings. It may also be built dynamically because it is a pure Python code. You make a Python module known as a URLconf to design URLs for an app (URL configuration). It easily maps the URL path expressions to Python functions (views).

HOW DOES IT PROCESS A REQUEST?

When a user requests for a page from your Django site, this is how the system follows the Python code to execute:

- It (Django) determines the root URLconf module to use.

- It loads the Python module and looks for the variable urlpatterns which can be defined in urls.py of the project. This should be a way to write Django.URLs.path().

- It runs through each URL pattern in order and stops at the first one that matches the requested URL, matching against path_info.

- When one of the URL patterns matches with your view, and the matched URL pattern contained no named groups, then the matches from the regular expression are provided as positional arguments.

WHAT IS URL ROUTING?

Before using the Regular Expressions to Django, we need to understand what URL routing is; it is actually pretty simple to understand. It is just a matter of how Django understands what the user is requesting.

These routes are called static routes.

Path	URL Route	View Name
http://example.com/	/	IndexPageView
http://example.com/about/	/about/	AboutPageView
http://example.com/user/id	/user/id/	UserIdView

What will these do?

- / - render the root page of the project.

- /about/- render the about page when user requests.

- /user/id- render the user with its id number. User will get to know the data whatever user is added.

These routes are called dynamic routes.

Path	URL Route	View Name
http://example.com/user/data/content	/user/data/content	UserDataContent
http://example.com/about/compan-name	/about/company-name	AboutCompanyView
http://example.com/user/id	/user/id/	UserIdView

The above examples are static routes in that they never change. The /about/ path will always be the /about/ path (unless we manually change it).

The handler (view) will be the exact same for both paths. The only way for the View (handler) to know which post to display, it must accept some additional values.

- The keyword arguments is where you give a name to a variable as you pass it into the function.

- django.URLs.path() or django.URLs.re_path().

In Django, we create dynamic URLs with path converters. A path converter has a simple syntax:

<type:variable>
There are five different path converter types:

1. **str**: matches any non-empty string, excluding '/'.

2. **path**: matches any non-empty string, including '/'. Useful for matching the entire URL.

3. **int**: matches an integer

4. **slug**: matches any slug string. E.g., slugs-are-text-strings-with-hy phens-and_underscores

5. **UUID**: matches a universally unique identifier (UUID)

This example has URL containing path converters:

- /<int:year>/<str:month>/

Let's put this into writing and modify this in urls.py for views function:

```
urlpatterns = [
  # path('', views.index, name='index'),
  path('<int:year>/<str:month>/', views.index,
name='index'),
]
```

WHAT IS PATH VS. RE_PATH?

To understand that the path function does not accept regex URLs anymore, you need to use the new URLs syntax <slug: title> instead of passing a regex through matching parameters. The re_path only works with regex formatted URLs (the old way we made URLs).

- If no URL pattern matches or exception is raised at any point in that process, Django invokes an appropriate error-handling view. See error handling below:
  "Is there various HTTP Status Code?"
  REST API Development with Node.js defines a status code as "a number that summarizes the response associated to it".

You can simply get the point that where is an error in it.

HTTP Status Number	Status
200	OK
201	Created
204	No content in returning
301	Content is moved from this URL.
400	Bad request means lack of parameter in URL
401	Forbidden (resource is not accessible)
404	Page not found
405	Method not allowed
500	Internal server error

Example:

```
from django.http import HttpResponse
def my_view(request):
    # ...
    # Return a "created" (201) response code.
    return HttpResponseNotFound('<h1>This page not
found</h1>')
```

- **Customizing error views:** The error views in Django can be easily overridden if you need any custom behavior. Some of the handlers are defined as follows:

    o The page_not_found() view is override by the handler404:handler404 = 'mysite.views.my_custom_page_not _found_view'

    o The server_error() view is override by the handler500: handler500 = 'mysite.views.my_custom_error_view'

    o The permission_denied() view is overrides by the handler403:handler400 = 'mysite.views.my_custom_bad_re quest_view'

    o handler403 = 'mysite.views.my_custom_permission_denied_vie w'

    o The bad_request() view is override by the handler400:

- **Returning errors in Django**

Class	Description
1. class HttpResponseNotModified	It is used to indicate that a page has not been modified since the user last request (status code 304)
2. class HttpResponseBadRequest	It is like HttpResponse but uses a 400 status code as an error
3. class HttpResponseNotFound	It is like HttpResponse but uses a 404 status code
4. class HttpResponseNotAllowed	It acts just like HttpResponse but uses a 410 status code
HttpResponseServerError	It acts just like HttpResponse but uses a 500 status code

- **Regular expressions:** It can be used as a compact way of specifying the pattern in the text. At the same time, Django allows regexes for URL matching. They relate to URLs.

Here's the same URLconf, rewritten to use non-named groups:

```
urlpatterns = [
    # Examples:
    re_path(r'^$', home_view, name='home_with_regex'),
    path("/", home_view, name='home_with_path'), #
same as the path above it.
    re_path(r'^contact/$', ContactView.as_view(),
name='contact'),
    re_path(r'^about/$', AboutView.as_view(),
name='about'),
    re_path(r'^profile/(?P<username>[\w.@+-]+)/$',
profile_detail, name='profile'),
    re_path(r'^article/(?P<slug>[\w-]+)/$', article_
detail, name='article'),
    re_path(r'^blog/', include("blog.urls")),
    re_path(r'^admin/', admin.site.urls),
]
```

For example, the non-named groups, a request to /student/2006/03/ would result in a function call equivalent to this:

- student_dob(request, '2006', '03')

Here is an example URLconf that uses named groups:

```
from django.conf.urls.defaults import *
from my site import views
urlpatterns = patterns('',
   (r'^route_name/(\d{4})/$', views.view_method),
   (r'^route_name/(\d{4})/(\d{2})/$', views.
view_method),
)
```

Symbol	Matches
. (dot)	Any single character
\d	Any single digit
[A-Z]	Any character between A and Z (uppercase)
[a-z]	Any character between a and z (lowercase)
[A-Za-z]	Any character between a and z (case-insensitive)
+	One or more of the previous expressions. For example, 1.\d+, It matches one or more digits
2.[^/]+	This includes one or more characters until (and not including) a forward slash
	3.? It denotes zero or one of the previous expressions. For example, \d? matches zero or one digits)
	4.* describes the zero or more of the previous expression (for example, \d* matches zero, one, or more than one digit)
{10,20}	Between 10 and 20 (inclusive) of the previous expression (for example, \d{2,5} matches two, three, four, five digits)

How to Create Views

Edit your views.py files and add an index function:

```
from Django. shortcuts import render
def index(request):
   return render(request, 'index.html')
```

Adding a Homepage Path

Edit your urls.py and add the index path to the URL patterns list:

```
from Django. contrib import admin
from Django.URLs import path
from myapp import views as myapp_views # < here
urlpatterns = [
```

```
path('admin/', admin.site.urls),
path('', myapp_views.index, name='index'), # < here
]
```

Now, run the development server:
```
python manage.py runserver
```

Function-Based Views

Let us have a brief look at function-based views and class-based views.

Function-based views are used by a beginner to easily understand that this will work as function. It is easy to understand in comparison to class-based views.

- It provides explicit code flow.

- It is a straightforward usage of decorators.

- But function-based view can't be extended and also leads to code redundancy.

Class-Based Views

This is special view that takes a request and returns a response. Django provides a few examples of some classes which can be used as views. These will allow you to restructure and reuse code for your views by harnessing inheritance and mixins.

- It supports the DRY convention of Django.

- We can enlarge class-based views and can add extra functionality according to our requirements using mixin.

- It allows inheriting methods and features from another class and can be modified for various use cases.

Examples:
All views inherit from the View class, which handles linking the view into the URLs, HTTP method dispatching, and other common features. RedirectView provides a HTTP redirect, and TemplateView extends the base class to make it also render a template.

- **Usage in your URL config**: The direct way to use generic views is to create them directly in your URLconf. If you're only changing a few attributes on a class-based view, you can pass them into the as_view() method call itself:

WHAT ARE GENERIC VIEWS?

It is an easy way to set those simple, complex views that are called generic views; the generic views are classes but not functions. Every generic view or class can be inherited. A set of classes for generic views are implemented as Django.views.generic.

. A

To get a command over class-based views, we have to use the as_view() in the urls.py file.

```
The class-based views are inherited.
# urls.py
from Django.URLs import path
from myapp.views import NewView
 urlpatterns = [
  path('about/', NewView.as_view()),
]
```

How to import generic view in code:
```
from Django.views.generic import ListView
```

Types of Generic View

1. **CreateView**: It implements the view to create an instance of a table in the database. It automatically does everything for creating a new instance. We only need to specify the name of the model to create a view and its fields.

```
from .models import Employee
from django.views.generic.edit import CreateView
 class EmployeeCreate(CreateView):
  model = Employee
    fields = '__all__'
```

2. **Retrieve View**: There are two types of retrieve view – first, the ListView refers to a view to display multiple instances of a table in database.

```
from django.views.generic.list import ListView
 class EmployeeRetrieve(ListView):
  model = Employee
```

3. **DetailView**: DetailView is slightly different from the ListView as it displays only one instance of a table in the database. Django automatically provides a primary key for each entry in the database, and we need to specify the <pk> in the request. DetailView will automatically perform everything.

```
from django.views.generic.detail import DetailView
 class EmployeeDetail(DetailView):
  model = Employee
```

4. **UpdateView**: It allows updating the single instance of the table from the database with some more details using id. It is used to alter the entries in the database.

```
from django.views.generic.edit UpdateView
class EmployeeDelete(UpdateView):
model = Employee
```

5. **DeleteView**: DeleteView allows deletion of the instance of a table from the database. It is used to delete the entries in the database.

```
from django.views.generic.edit DeleteView
class EmployeeDelete(DeleteView):
model = Employee
```

Django View HTTP Decorators

These HTTP Decorators are used to restrict the path to view based on the request method. These decorators are listed in Django.views.decorators.HTTP.

A decorator is a dynamically altered function that takes other functions as its argument and returns another further function. It can be extremely useful as they allow the extension of an existing function without any modification to the original function source code. A good example of the decorator is that we can declare it before the view as @login_required. But Django returns a newer version of the function.

Syntax: require_http_methods(request_method_list)

```
from django.shortcuts import render
# Create your views here.
from django.http import HttpResponse,
HttpResponseNotFound
from django.views.decorators.http import
require_http_methods
@require_http_methods(["GET"])
def index(request):
  return HttpResponse('<h1> Http GET request using @
require_http_method.</h1>')
#url.py
from django.contrib import admin
from django.urls import path
from myapp import views
urlpatterns = [
  path('admin/', admin.site.urls),
  path('index/', views.index),
  path('show/', views.show),
]
```

URLconfs and Loose Coupling

In a Django app, the URL definitions and the view functions both are called loosely coupled.

```
urlpatterns = [
url('admin/', include(admin.site.urls)),
url(r^hello/$', hello),
url(r'^time/$', current_datetime),
url(r'^another-time-page/$', current_datetime),
]
```

Django Exceptions and Error-Handling

```
def hours_ahead(request, offset):
  try:
    offset = int(offset)
  except ValueError:
    raise Http404()
  dt = datetime.datetime.now() + datetime.
timedelta(hours=offset)
  assert False
```

```
html = "In %s hour(s), it will be %s." % (offset,
dt)
    return HttpResponse(html)
```

If we comment on the few lines of the above code or miss the few words in the code, the Error will occur. We can debug our error.

There can be numerous errors in our applications, websites, and programs. Error-handling is an important skill. It is a must for all developers. You should have some hand-on experience with exception-handling in Python code.

WHAT ARE EXCEPTIONS?

These are those events in a program whose occurrence can lead to an unwanted behavior. They are able to detect errors by run-time executive or operating system. Exceptions do not always emerge from errors. Errors can only be caught, and a response can be generated only when all can be done. Exceptions are the only thing that the developers actually deal with every single day.

Exception in Python

This part of this book offers exceptions, which are events that can modify the flow of control through a program. They are processed by the following five statements:

1. **try/except**: It matches and recovers from exceptions raised by code, or by you.

2. **try/finally**: It performs cleanup actions in the code, whether exceptions occur or not.

3. **Raise**: It triggers an exception manually by the programmer in their code.

4. **Assert**: It conditionally triggers an exception in your code and the condition is evaluated to True results.

5. **With/as**: It implements context managers in Python 2.6 and 3.0.

This topic was saved until nearly the end of this book because you need to know about it.

WHY PRACTICE EXCEPTIONS?

An exception is a simple event that occurs during the execution of a program that disturbs the normal flow of the program. In general, when a Python script finds a situation that it cannot cope with, it puts an exception. An exception is a Python object that represents an error.

Common Exception

The following is a list of common exceptions:

- **ZeroDivisionError**: This error occurs when a number is divided by zero.

  1. **NameError**: It occurs when a name is not found. It may be local or global.

  2. **IndentationError**: If incorrect, indentation is given.

  3. **IOError**: It only occurs when input and output operation fails.

  4. **EOFError**: It occurs when the end of the file is reached, and yet operations are being performed.

Syntax:

```
try:
 #block of code
 except Exception1:
 #block of code
 except Exception2:
 #block of code
 #other code
```

Example:

```
try:
 a = int(input("Enter a:"))
 b = int(input("Enter b:"))
 c = a/b
except:
 print("Can't divide with zero")
```

Example:

```
try :{
}
except:{
}
else:{
}
finally:{
}
```

Explanation

1. **try-expect statement**: In any Python program code, using this code is useful because the try block only contains the running code. If this code is not working properly, then execution will be terminated, and it will throw an error to the except block. It is always preceded by a try keyword.

2. **except statement**: The except block always declares a type of exception that it handles using the exception variable.

   We can use the exception variable name with the except statement along with the keyword. The Python language allows us to declare the multiple exceptions with the except clause one at a time.

3. **try-finally block**: Python will be the optional statement, which is used only with the try statement. It defines a block of code to run the try block. It does not execute matter that exception raises. The final block gives a guarantee of the execution, meaning it will always run any kind of error that occurs or not.

Raising Exceptions

It can be raised forcefully by using the raise clause in the code. It is useful in such a scenario where we need to raise an exception to stop the execution of the program where you want.

```
raise Exception_class <value>
```

Custom Exceptions

The Python allows us to create our own exceptions that can be raised by the program and caught using the except clause.

```
try:
  a = int(input("Enter a:"))
  b = int(input("Enter b:"))
  c = a/b;
  print("a/b = %d"%c)
except:
  print("can't divide by zero")
else:
  print("Hi I am else block")
```

Let us learn how Django raises the different kinds of exceptions in code.

Django Exceptions

- **Django.core. Exceptions Package**: This will provide us with low-level errors and will also allow us to define a new set of rules for our Django project. We can also load models and views in our own ways.

This module has use-cases example:

- When you will be working on custom Middleware.

- When making some changes to Django ORM.

```
from django.core import exceptions
list_errors = list(dir(exceptions))
for i in list_errors:
  print(i)
AppRegistryNotReady
BadRequest
DisallowedHost
DisallowedRedirect
EmptyResultSet
FieldDoesNotExist
FieldError
ImproperlyConfigured
MiddlewareNotUsed
MultipleObjectsReturned
NON_FIELD_ERRORS
ObjectDoesNotExist
PermissionDenied
```

```
RequestAborted
RequestDataTooBig
SuspiciousFileOperation
SuspiciousMultipartForm
SuspiciousOperation
SynchronousOnlyOperation
TooManyFieldsSent
ValidationError
ViewDoesNotExist
__builtins__
__cached__
__doc__
__file__
__loader__
__name__
__package__
__spec__
make_hashable
operator
```

1. **AppRegistryNotReady**: When the Django project runs, it generates an application registry. It has the information related to it in your settings.py and some more custom settings. This registry will keep track of your record and install all the important components in your project – This exception arises when we attempt to use the model before the app loading.

2. **ObjectDoesNotExist**: This will occur when we request an object which does not exist in the code. It is the base class for DoesNotExist Errors.ObjectDoesNotExist that emerges mainly from get() in Django. get() is an important method used to return data from the server. This method returns the object when found.

3. **EmptyResultSet**: This is rare because most of the queries return something as a result. It only runs when there is nothing to return as a result.

4. **FieldDoesNotExist**: The Meta.get_field() function connects views and models. Django uses this method to search the fields when the model objects are in view functions. This method also searches super_models for the requested field. It becomes helpful once we've done some model adjustments.

5. **MultipleObjectsReturned**: Models also have a MultipleObjectsReturned property. Some models need many items to be returned, whereas others cannot have more than one. This exception allows us to have additional control over the data in the model.

6. **SuspiciousOperation**; It is one of Django's security classes. When Django detects harmful behavior from the user, it raises this error. This exception contains a lot of subclasses that can help you improve your security.

   There are several subclasses that deal with extremely specific issues:

   - DisallowedHost

   - DisallowedModelAdminLookup

   - DisallowedModelAdminToField

   - DisallowedRedirect

   - InvalidSessionKey

   - RequestDataTooBig

   - SuspiciousFileOperation

   - SuspiciousMultipartForm

   - SuspiciousSession

   - TooManyFieldsSent

7. **PermissionDenied**: When we store our static files in an inaccessible location, Django throws this issue. You may raise this using the try/except block, but the static files method is more fun. Change the static folder settings to hidden or protected to increase it.

8. **ViewDoesNotExist**: This is something we've all been through. Websites' frontend designs are constantly changing, and frequent changes might result in erroneous URLs. By default, Django checks for all URLs and view functions. The server will display an error if something is incorrect.

9. **MiddlewareNotUsed**: When an unused middleware is present in the MIDDLEWARES list, it throws this exception. It is similar to

middleware for caching. This exception will be thrown whenever we haven't installed caching on our website.

10. **FieldError**: When models include mistakes, we raise field errors.

Examples include fields in a model having the same name.

Infinite loops result from incorrect ordering.

Methods of join and drop are being used incorrectly.

It is possible that the names of the fields don't exist, and so forth.

11. **ValidationError**: When models include mistakes, we raise field errors.

Examples include fields in a model having the same name.

Infinite loops result from incorrect ordering.

Methods of join and drop are being used incorrectly.

It is possible that the names of the fields don't exist, and so forth.

URL Resolver Exceptions

Django. URLs is one of Django's basic classes, and it wouldn't work without it. There are a few exceptions to this class:

1. **Resolver404**: If path() does not have a valid view to map, this exception is thrown. The error page is displayed by Resolver404. It's a subclass of the Django.HTTP.Http404 module.

2. **NoReverseMatch**: When we request a URL that is not defined in our URLs-config, we get this error.

3. **Database Exceptions**: Django's exception wrappers function in the same way as the Python database API.

The errors are:

• InterfaceError

• DatabaseError

• DataError

• IntegrityError

- InternalError

- ProgrammingError

- NotSupportedError

We raise these errors when:

- The database is not found

- The interface is not there

- The database is not connected

- Input data is not valid, etc.

4. **HTTP Exceptions**: Django's HttpResponse class is a subclass. HTTP is a kind of protocol. Exceptions and specific answers are provided by the module.

5. **Transaction Exceptions**: A sequence of database queries is referred to as a transaction. It is where you'll find the tiniest queries, also known as atomic queries. When an error occurs at this atomic level, the Django.DB.transaction module resolves it.

6. **Testing Framework Exceptions**: The Django. test package also comes with many exceptions.

ADVANCED VIEW AND URLS

This is the older way to define views and URLs.

```
from django.conf.urls.defaults import *
urlpatterns = patterns('',
    (r'^index/$', 'mysite.views.indx'),
    (r'^index/$', 'myapp.views.currentdatetime'),
    (r'^index/plus/(\d{1,2})/$', 'myapp.views.hours'),
    (r'^tag/(\w+)/$', 'blog.views.tag'),
)
```

The new way is as follows:

```
from django.conf.urls.defaults import *
urlpatterns = patterns('mysite.views',
    (r'^time/$', 'hello'),
    (r'^time/$', 'current_datetime'),
```

```
  (r'^time/plus/(\d{1,2})/$', 'hours'),
)
urlpatterns += patterns('blog.views',
  (r'^tag/(\w+)/$', 'tag'),
)
```

The framework is only concerned with the existence of a module-level variable named URL patterns. As seen in this example, this variable may be created dynamically. It is worth noting that the objects provided by patterns() can be joined together, something you might not expect.

Using Named Groups

We've used simple, non-named regular expression groups in all of our URLconf examples so far – that is, we place parentheses around bits of the URL we wish to capture, and Django provides the captured text to the view function as a positional parameter. It is possible to utilize named regular expression groups to capture URL bits and give them as keyword arguments to a view in more advanced use.

Keyword Arguments vs. Positional Arguments

Keyword arguments or positional arguments can be used to invoke a Python function, and in certain situations both at the same time. You define the names of the arguments as well as the values you're sending in a keyword argument call. In a positional argument call, you just send the arguments without saying which argument corresponds to which value; the relationship is implied by the sequence of the arguments.

Passing Extra Options to View Functions

Sometimes you will find yourself that view functions are quite similar:

```
# urls.py
from django.conf.urls.defaults import *
from mysite import views
urlpatterns = patterns('',
  (r'^foo/$', views.foo_view),
  (r'^bar/$', views.bar_view),
)

from Django. shortcuts import render
from my site. models import MyModelname
```

```
def foo_view(request):
  m_list = MyModelName.objects.filter(is_new=True)
  return render(request, 'template1.html', {'m_
list': list})
def bar_view(request):
  m_list = MyModelName.objects.filter(is_new=True)
  return render(request, 'template2.html', {'m_
list': m_list})
```

CHAPTER SUMMARY

In this chapter, we have covered in detail Django's views, beginning with the basics of Django views, how the views interact with models and templates and the rest of the project. To help you understand views at a beginner level, we showed you how they work using simple HTML responses. In the next chapter, we'll cover the fundamentals of Django's templates.

## CHAPTER 6

Django's Templates

IN THIS CHAPTER

➤ Getting to know about Django's templates

➤ Templating engine Jinja

➤ Loaders

➤ Static files

In the last chapter, we learned about Django's models with their implementation, syntax, models package, primary admin interface, and type of database where data is stored.

In this chapter, we will discuss how the data renders in your Django project using templates. We will leaWrn about template engines like Jinja2, template inheritance, some in-built Python functions; all with proper explanations. Now it's time to get into it.

BASICS OF TEMPLATE

The templates in Django are strings of indented text to separate the presentation of a document from its data. It is the template that defines placeholders and various bits of basic logic that regulate how the paper should be displayed. Templates are used for showing HTML, but Django templates are equally capable of text-based format data.

Let's review a simple example of a template. Signifying a web framework, Django needs a convenient way to generate HTML dynamically. The most common approach relies on templates.

DOI: 10.1201/9781003310495-6

119

A Django project can be worked with one or more several templates. Django has its in-built backend for its own templates system; it is called Django template language (DTL), a popular alternative is Jinja2. Backends for the other template language can be available from third parties. We can also write a custom backend.

First, we will talk about the Jinja template briefly.

JINJA

Jinja is also commonly referred to as "Jinja2". The Python templating engine is used to create HTML, XML, or other markup formats returned to the user via an HTTP response. It is a fast, expressive, extensible templating engine. These templates allow writing code similar to Python syntax. This template is then passed data to render the final document.

Why Is Jinja2 Useful?

It has consistent template tag syntax, and the project is cleanly extracted as independent and open-source by other code libraries.

Origin of Jinja2?

It is not the only template engine that exists. Django's built-in template engine inspires Jinja2's syntax. Many template systems, such as JavaServer Pages (JSPs), originated many years before Jinja. You should know the fundamental of Jinja2 before starting to use it. It is built upon the concepts of other template engines, and nowadays it is widely used by the Python community and developers.

API

This will define the API to Jinja and not the template language. Let's talk about the basics of it. It uses an object called the template. The class instances are used to store the global things and used to load templates from the file system or other locations.

The simplest way to configure Jinja is to load templates.

```
from jinja2 import Environment, PackageLoader,
select_autoescape
env = Environment(
  loader=PackageLoader("Your_app_name"),
  autoescape=select_autoescape()
)
```

This will create a template environment with a loader that looks up templates in the templates folder inside the 'Your_app_name' Python package (or next to the Your_app_name.py Python module). It also enables autoescaping for HTML files. It might allow autorunning by default for security reasons.

Why do we need Jinja2?

1. It provides protected framework for testing programs whose behavior is unknown and must be investigated.

2. It has a powerful automatic HTML Escaping feature, which helps the site prevent Cross-site Scripting (XSS Attack).

3. There are special characters like >, <, &, and so on that carry special meanings in the templates.

4. It has a most important feature which will expand your project, that is Template Inheritance.

5. It consists of extensible filters, tests, functions, and more clear syntax.

6. It makes debugging easier.

7. These are compiled to optimize Python code just in time.

8. I18N support with Babel.

9. Define and import macros within templates.

Installation
If you want to install Jinja in your system, you require Python 3.6 and a newer version of Python. Run this command in the terminal as follows:

```
pip install Jinja2
# another way to add Jinja to your project
pip install jinja2
easy_install jinja2
```

Dependencies
These will automatically be installed when installing Jinja.

- **Markup Safe**: It escapes the untrusted when rendering the templates to avoid malicious attacks.

- **Babel**: It provides translation support in Jinja templates.

WHAT IS BABEL?

It provides a message extraction framework. This package contains various messages for integration.

- A message extraction plugin for Django templates: Django-Babel comes with a method plugin that can extract messages from Django template files. Python is supported entirely by Babel.

- A middleware class that adds the Babel Locale_object to requests: To use the Babel middleware, make sure you add it to the list of MIDDLEWARE_CLASSES in your settings module.

```
MIDDLEWARE_CLASSES = (
   . . .
   'django.middleware.locale.LocaleMiddleware',
   'django_babel.middleware.LocaleMiddleware',
   . . .
)
```

- Template tags for date and number formatting: To make the template filters/tags available in your project, you need to add Django-Babel to the list of INSTALLED_APPS in your settings module:

```
INSTALLED_APPS = (
   . . .
   'django_babel',
   . . .
)
```

Jinja supports the latest version, Python 3.4, and newer. We also recommend using a virtual environment in order to add dependencies from other projects and the system.

Template

It represents the syntax and semantics of the template engine. The template engine is so flexible that the application's configuration can be different from the code presented here.

The template is simply a text file. Jinja can generate any text-based format like HTML, XML, etc. It does not need to have a specific extension: .html, .xml, etc. It contains variables and/or expressions, which get replaced with values when a template is rendered, and tags, which control the logic. Django and Python inspire this.

A few examples will help to understand the default behavior of the Jinja configuration.

```
<!doctype html>
<html lang="en">
 <head>
  <title>Title</title>
  <!-- Required meta tags -->
  <meta charset="utf-8">
  <meta name="viewport" content="width=device-width,
initial-scale=1, shrink-to-fit=no">
  <link rel="stylesheet" href="{% static 'css/style
.css' %}">
  <!-- Bootstrap CSS -->
  <link rel="stylesheet" href="https://stackpath
.bootstrapcdn.com/bootstrap/4.3.1/css/bootstrap.min
.css">
  <link rel="stylesheet" href="https://cdnjs
.cloudflare.com/ajax/libs/font-awesome/5.12.1/css/
all.min.css">
 </head>
 <body>
  {% block content %}
  <!DOCTYPE html>
  <html lang="en">
  <head>
    <title>My Webpage</title>
  </head>
  <body>
    <ul id="navigation">
    {% for item in items %}
      <li><a href="{{ item.href }}">{{ item.caption
}}</a></li>
    {% endfor %}
    </ul>
     <h1>My Webpage</h1>
    {{ name_of_website }}
     {# a comment #}
  </body>
  </html>
  {% endblock %}
  <!-- Optional JavaScript -->
  <!-- jQuery first, then Popper.js, then Bootstrap
JS -->
```

```
<script src="https://code.jquery.com/jquery-3.3.1
.slim.min.js" ></script>
<script src="https://stackpath.bootstrapcdn.com/
bootstrap/4.3.1/js/bootstrap.min.js"></script>
</body>
</html>
```

In the above example, you see everything related to the templates in Django. Don't get confused after looking at this code, and we will explain each and every step of the code. Let's look at it.

Start your HTML code and then write the common boilerplate and add on your additional files in the <head> tag of CSS in <link> tag. After that, we will see {% block content %}. The following example shows syntax configuration.

Django Template System Basic

A *template tag* is surrounded by {% and %}. This is because Django's tags are so flexible. Some examples performed by template tags are as follows:

1. **Display Logic:** E.g., {% if %} Add {% endif %}

2. **Loop Control:** E.g., {% for x in y %}...{% endfor %}

3. **Block Declaration:** E.g., {% block content %}...{% endblock %}

4. **Content Import:** E.g., {% include "header.html" %}

5. **Inheritance:** E.g., {% extends "base.html" %}

A template variable is surrounded by {{ and }}. These template variables are passed to the template at runtime in the Context.

1. **Simple Variables:** E.g., {{ name }}

2. **Object Attributes:** E.g., {{ page.heading }}

3. **Dictionary Lookups:** E.g., {{ dict.item }}

4. **List Indexes:** E.g., {{ list_items.2 }}

5. **Method Calls:** E.g., {{ var.lower }}, {{ mydict.push }}

There are few delimiters as follows:

- **Display Logic - {% ... %} (for Statements):** A control statement refers to all those things that control the flow of a program – conditionals if/elif/else, for-loops, as well as things like macros and blocks. Example,

```
<h1>Favorite Color</h1>
<ul>
{% for user in colors %}
 <li>{{ user.color }}</li>
{% endfor %}
</ul>
```

- **If:** In Jinja, it is easiest to use if as a variable that is defined and then returns some values, not empty and not false.

```
{% if users %}
<ul>
{% for user in users %}
  <li>{{ user.username}}</li>
{% endfor %}
</ul>
{% endif %}
#Template will get value from view.py in form of
dictionary.
{'users':user})
```

- **If Expression:** It is also used as an inline expression. For example, you can add this to extend your code logic.

```
{% extends condition if the condition is defined
else 'default.html' %}
```

- o **Expressions:** It allows expression everywhere. The simplest form of expression is literals. They are represented as Python objects such as strings and numbers. The following are literals:

  - **"Django with Python":** Single quotes or double quote works as same.

  - **123 / 123_432:** Integers are whole numbers without decimal parts.

  - **12.12:** Floating pint number can be written as a decimal mark.

- ['**List**', '**of**', '**objects**']: Everything define in between [] these is list. It is used to store data in a sequential manner.

- ('**Values**', '**of**', '**tuples**'): Tuples are like that cannot be modified ("immutable list"). It is usually used to represent items of two or more elements.

- {'**Key**": "**Value**"} = In Python dictionary is a structure that includes the keys and values represented as Key values pairs. The keys must be unique and always have exactly one value. It is rarely used in the template.

- **True/false:** true is always true, and false is always false. True, false, and none should be in lowercase.

Operators

Math   Jinja allows you to calculate with values.

- **(+):** Adds two instances together. Usually, the objects are numbers, but they also add both strings or lists to add the extra data. Example: {{ 1+1 }} is 2.

- **(−):** It subtracts the second number from the first one. {{ 3 - 2 }} is 1.

- **(/):** It will divide two numbers and return value will be a floating point number. {{ 1 / 2 }} is {{ 0.5 }}.

- **(%):** Calculate the remainder of an integer division. {{ 11 % 7 }} is 4.

- **(*):** Multiply the left operand with the right one. {{ 2 * 2 }} would return 4 and it may also be used to repeat a string multiple times. {{ '=' * 4 }} would print a bar of 80 equal signs ****.

- **(**):** Raise the left operand to the power of the right operand. {{ 2**3 }} would return 8.

Other Operators

- **in:** It returns true if the left operand exists in the right. {{ 2 in [1, 2, 3,,4] }} would, for example, return true.

- **Is:** Used to perform tests.

- **| (a pipe, vertical):** Used to apply filter.

- **~ (tilde):** Converts all operands into strings and concatenates them.

Python in-built Method

Python has various in-built methods. You can also use any of the methods defined on a variable type.

abs()	xmlattr ()	jsonencode()	round()	lower()
float()	format()	pprint()	join()	trim()
slice()	truncate()	capitalize()	string()	reverse()
dformat()	center()	int()	urlencode()	sort()
replace()	length()	upper()	random()	dictsort()
last()	wordcount()	sum()	first()	list()
title()	filesizeformat()	escape()	trim()	urlize()

- **Explanation:** Templates are a way to filter the alternating value of the variable before they are displayed. Filters use a pipe character like this. {{ name | lower }}

Various Functions

- **abs**: It will return the absolute value of the number as an argument. For example, if a variable contains –15, the filter statement {{variable| abs}} outputs 15.

- **xmlattr**: It will create an SGML/XML attribute string, but it depends on the items in a dict. All values, neither none nor undefined, are automatically escaped.

- **JSON encode**: JSON dumps a variable, it just works if a simple JSON is installed.

- **round**: It filter rounds a number to a given precision, where the first argument is the precision – which defaults to 0.
  - o 'common' rounds either up or down
  - o 'ceil' always rounds up
  - o 'floor' always rounds down

- **lower**: It will convert all values of a string variable to a lowercase character. For example, if a variable contains Hello Python, the filter statement {{variable | lower}} outputs hello Python.

- **float**: It will filter convert a value into a floating-point number.

- **Print**: It is a variable useful for debugging.

- **Join**: It will return a string which is the concatenation of the strings in the sequence.

- **Trim**: The trim filter is used to strip leading and trailing whitespace just like Python's string strip() Method.

- **Slice**: It will provide an iterator and return a list of lists containing those items.

- **Truncate**: Return a truncated copy of the string.

- **Capitalize**: This filter capitalizes the first letter of a string variable. For example, if a variable contains hello Python, the filter statement {{variable | capitalize}} outputs Hello Python.

- **String**: The string filter makes a string Unicode if it isn't already.

- **Reverse**: Return a reversed list of the sequence filtered.

- **Format**: Apply Python mapping string formatting on an object.

- **Center**: It center aligns a value and pads it with additional white space characters until it reaches the given argument of characters.

- **Int**: The int filter converts a value into an integer.

- **urlencode**: It will escape a value for use in URLs. For example, variable contains http://localhost/data?type=cold&size=large the filter statement {{variable| urlencode }} outputs http%3A//localhost/data%3Ftype%3Dcold%26size%3Dlarge.

- **sort**: Sort a sequence. By default, it sorts ascending, and if you pass it True as the first argument, it will reverse the sorting.

- **Replace**: It will work just like Python replace string. The first part of the sub-string should be replaced; the second is the replacement string.

- **Length**: Return the length of the value.

- **Upper**: It will convert all values of a string of letters to uppercase. For example, if a variable contains Hello Python, the filter statement {{variable| upper}} outputs HELLO PYTHON.

- **Random**: It will return a random item from the sequence.

- **dictsort**: It will sort a dict and yield (key, value) pairs. Because the dictionary is unsorted, you may want to use this function to order them.

- **Last**: Return the last item of a sequence.

- **sum**: It will return the sum of a sequence of numbers, plus the value provided with the start parameter, which defaults to 0.

- **first**: Return the first item of a sequence.

- **List**: It will be used to return a list of characters. For example, a variable contains a letter and the filter statement {{variable | list}} generates ['la, 'v','b','t', 's'].

- **title**: It will convert all first character values of a string letter to uppercase. For example, if a variable contains Hello Python, the filter statement {{variable| title}} outputs Hello Python.

- **file size format**: It will convert a number of bytes into a friendly file size string. For example, if a variable contains 150, the filter statement {{variable| filesizeformat}} outputs 150 bytes.

- **escape**: It escapes HTML characters from a value. Specifically, with the escape filter,

  1. < is converted to <
  2. > is converted to >,
  3. ' (single quote) is converted to '
  4. " (double quote) is converted to &quot,
  5. & is converted to &amp.

- **Trim**: It is used to strip leading and trailing whitespace just like Python's string strip() method.

- **urlize**: It will make your text URLs into clickable HTML links.

Comparisons

- (==): Compares two objects for equality.

- (!=): Compares two objects for inequality.

- (>): True if the left-hand side is greater than the right-hand side.

- (>=): True if the left-hand side is greater or equal to the right-hand side.

- (<): The left-hand side is lower than the right-hand side.

- (<=): The left-hand side is lower than or equal to the right-hand side value.

Logic

If statements, filtering, and if expressions can be useful to combine multiple expressions:

1. (**and**): Return true if the left and the right operand are true.

2. (**Or**): Return true if the left or the right operand is true.

3. (**not**): negate a statement (see below).

4. **(expr):** Parentheses group an expression.

Rendering a Template

When you have a Template object, you can pass its data by giving it a context:

```
from django.template import Context, Template
obj_t = Template('You are learning {{ name }}.')
obj_c = Context({'name': 'Python with Django'})
t.render(c)
```

A context is a similar to a set of template variable names and their values. A template uses a context to populate its variables. A context in Django is represented by the Context class. The Template object's render() method with the Context is called to "fill" the template. We should point out here that the return value of obj_t.render(obj_c) is a Unicode object – not a normal Python string.

Let's step into this code one statement at a time:

- First, we import the Template and Context classes, which are available in the module, which is Django. Template.

- We pass the raw text of our template into some variable.

- Next we create a template object, obj_t, by passing raw_template to the Template class constructor.

- We create a Context object, obj_c. A Context is an object that takes a Python dictionary, which maps variable names to values.

- Eventually, we can call the render() method on our template object by passing it the Context.

The Django Template Language

- **Variable:** It has to output a value from the Context, which is a direct-like object mapping keys to values. Variables are surrounded by {{ and }} like this:

   o I am learning {{ name1 }} with{ name2 }}.

   o With a context of {'name1': 'Python', 'name2': 'Django'}, output like:

   o I am learning Python with Django.

Having dictionary lookup, attribute lookup and list-index lookups are implemented with a dot notation(.):

- {{ my_own_dict.key }}

- {{ my_own_object.attribute }}

- {{ my_own_list.0 }}

Tags: It provides an arbitrary logic in the rendering process. Tags can output the content, e.g., an "if" statement or a "for" loop, etc.

Tags are surrounded by {% and %}.

```
{% csrf_token %} #used for authentication purpose
in <form> tag.
```

Filter: It transforms the values of variable and tag arguments. They look like this:

```
{{ django|title }}
```

We have various filters:
add: Adds the argument to the value.

```
{{ value|add:"2" }} #If value is "django", the
output will be "Django".
```

center: The value is a field of a given width.

```
{{ value|center:"2" }} #If value is "Django", the
output will be " Django ".
```

Other filters are as follows:

- date

- cut

- default

- dictsort

- divisible by

- dictsortreversed and many more.

WHY DO WE USE ENGINE?

Django Template: The engine is an instance of the Django template system. Benefits of using Jinja:

- **Speed and performance**: It compiles template source code to Python bytecode when it is loaded, so the template is only parsed, resulting in better performance at runtime.

- **Similar to the Django template**: It is actually inspired by Django templates, so there is a lot of common ground between the two systems.

- **Asynchronous execution**: Jinja templates support asynchronous execution, which allows backing tasks to run their course – without holding back templates.

- **Flexibility**: They can contain supporting concepts like macros and more Python-like constructs.

WHAT ARE LOADERS?

Template loaders are responsible for locating the template and returning template objects.

Support for Template Engines

Configuration or How Django Finds the Templates?

Templates engines are configured in the TEMPLATES setting. It is a list of all the configurations, one for each engine.

```
TEMPLATES = [
  {
    'BACKEND': 'django.template.backends.django.Dj
angoTemplates',
    'DIRS': ['template'],
    'APP_DIRS': True,
    'OPTIONS': {
      'context_processors': [
        'django.template.context_processors.debug',
        'django.template.context_processors.request',
        'django.contrib.auth.context_processors.a
uth',
        'django.contrib.messages.context_processo
rs.messages',
      ],
    },
  },
]
```

Backend dotted Python path to a template class: The built-in backends are 'Django.template.backends.Django.DjangoTemplates'.

Common terms used in TEMPLATE

- **DIRS**: It is the list of directories where the engine should look.

- **APP_DIRS**: It tells whether the engine should look for a template inside the application. When it is True, Django Templates engines look for template and then the template engine looks at the templates subdirectory of installed applications.

Creating a Site Template

Django did not create the \templates folder for you, so create it by own. When you are finished, your folder structure should look like this:

```
\myclub_site # You App Folder
  \templates #Your Template Folder
```

```
__init__.py #Template files
...
```

Addition Path for Template

os.path.join is a Python command to create a file path by joining strings together. In this example, we are joining my site/templates to our project directory to create the full path to our templates directory, i.e., <your project path>/root/my site/templates.

```
TEMPLATES = [
  {
    'BACKEND': 'django.template.backends.django.Dj
angoTemplates',
    'DIRS': ['template'],
    'APP_DIRS': os.path.join(BASE_DIR, 'mysite/
templates'),
    'OPTIONS': {
      'context_processors': [
        'django.template.context_processors.debug',
        'django.template.context_processors.request',
        'django.contrib.auth.context_processors.a
uth',
        'django.contrib.messages.context_processo
rs.messages',
      ],
    },
  },
]
```

Full Example of Templates

You can add a template in setting.py like above.

```
#views.py
def index(request):
  data = " I am learning ".
  return render(request,'index.html',{'data': data})
#index.html
<html>
 <head>
  <title></title>
 </head>
```

```
<body>
<!-- Data will render here -->
{{data}}
</body>
</html>
#urls.py
urlpatterns = [
  path('', index,name="index"),
]
```

Render() is a special Django helper function that creates a shortcut for communicating with a web browser.

Class Jinja2
It is necessary to install:

```
>>> python -m pip install Jinja2
```

Set BACKEND to ' Django.template.backend.jinaj2.Jinja2 ' to use Jinja2 engine.

The most important entry in OPTIONS is 'environment.' It is a Python path to callable returning a Jinja environment. Django will add defaults that differ from Jinja2's for
options.

There are few common notations used in Django:

1. **"autoescape"**: True

2. **"loader"**: a loader configured for DIRS and APSS_DIRS.

3. **"auto_reload"**: setting.DEBUG

4. **"undefined"**: DebugUndefined is settings.DEBUG else Undefined.

Usage of Template Loaders
The Django.template.loader module is loaders modules that define two functions to load templates:

- **get_template(template_name, using=None):** This function loads the template with the given name and returns a Template object. If any template cannot be found, it raises the TemplateDoesNotExist error. If the template exists but contains invalid syntax, it raises TemplateSyntaxError error.

- **select_template(template_name_list, using=None):** It is just like get_template(), it takes a list of template names. It will try each name in order and return the first template that exists.

Optional Argument

- **Backend**: It is an instance from which the exception originated.

- **Tried**: A list of sources that were tried when finding the template formatted as a list of tuples containing (origin, status).

- **Chain**: This is used by functions, such as get_template(), that try to load a given template from multiple engines.

Example:

```
TEMPLATES = [
  {
    'BACKEND': 'django.template.backends.django.Dj
angoTemplates',
    'DIRS': [
      '/home/html/example.com',
      '/home/html/default',
    ],
  },
  {
    'BACKEND': 'django.template.backends.jinja2.Ji
nja2',
    'DIRS': [
      '/home/html/jinja2',
    ],
  },
]
```

Template Inheritance

Jinja2 supports template inheritance, which is the most powerful, useful feature of any templating engine. It means that one template can inherit from another template.

Almost each and every website has a navigation bar attached to the top of its page. Repeating the code is a bad idea, so to avoid repeating the code, we use the inheritance feature because it saves a lot more time and also reduces work.

A base page template contains the basic layout, which is common to all the other templates. This base template extends or derives the layout for other pages.

Example: We have a parent template.

```
<!DOCTYPE html>
<html>
<head>
 {% block head %}
 <title>{% block title %}{% endblock %}</title>
 {% endblock %}
</head>
<body>
 {% block body %}{% endblock %}
</body>
</html>
```

Template inheritance {% block %}: This tag is used to tell the template engine that we want to override the common elements of our site via some common templates. It is the parent template which is the basic layout and on which you can modify using the child templates.

Example: We have a child template in it; we are going to extend our cord with the bits of help extends.

```
{% extends "base.html" %}
{% block title %} Index {% endblock %}
{% block head %}
 {{ super() }}
{% endblock %}
{% block body %}
 <h1>Hello World</h1>
 <p>Welcome to my site.</p>
{% endblock %}
```

1. The {% extend %} must be the very first tag in the child templates. This tag tells the template engine that this template extends from the parent template or (base.html).

2. {% extend %} represents the inheritance.

Django Static Files Handling

Django deals with it efficiently and provides a convenient manner to use its resources. The Django.contrib.static files module helps to manage all the static files.

Django Static (CSS, JavaScript, images) Configuration:

- Includes the django.contrib.staticfiles in INSTALLED_APPS.

- Defines STATIC_URL in settings.py file as given below:

- STATIC_URL = '/static/'

- Loads the static files in the templates by using the below expression:

- {% load static %}

- Stores all the images, JavaScript, CSS files in a static folder of the application and then creates a directory static and store the files inside it.

To load your static files in a template, add the below code in your base.ht ml in the beginning. You can then get access to your static folder. In the static folder, you can keep your CSS, JavaScript, and Bootstrap files.

- **Django Image Loading Example**:

```
<!DOCTYPE html>
<html lang="en">
<head>
  <meta charset="UTF-8">
  <title>Index</title>
    {% load static %}
</head>
<body>
<img src="{% static '/wallpaper.jpeg' %}"
alt="image" height="200px" width="500px"/>
</body>
</html>
```

- **Django Loading JavaScript**: To load JavaScript code in your file, just add the following line of code in index.html file:

To load JavaScript code in your file, just add the following line of code in index.html file:
{% load static %}

- <script src="{% static '/js/script.js' %}"

```
<!DOCTYPE html>
<html lang="en">
<head>
  <meta charset="UTF-8">
  <title>Index</title>
    {% load static %}
    <script src="{% static '/js/script.js' %}"
type="text/javascript"></script>
</head>
<body>
</body>
</html>
```

- **Django Loading CSS Example**:

```
{% load static %}
<!DOCTYPE html>
<html lang="en">
<head>
  <meta charset="UTF-8">
  <title>Index Page</title>
  <link href="{% static 'css/style.css' %}"
rel="stylesheet">
</head>
<body>
<p> I am Learning Python with Django </p>
</body>
</html>
```

- **Use of Forms in html Templating**:

```
<form method="POST" enctype="multipart/form-data">
  {% csrf_token %}
  {{ formset.as_p }}
  <input type="submit" value="Submit">
</form>
```

We create an HTML page for our website in which we have used <form> tag with some attributes like Method that means method to get and send with the help of Types of Method we have:

- GET

GET is used to request (getting) data from a resource. It is one of the most common HTTP methods.

How it looks like in the URL:

- /test/demo_site.php?name1=value1&name2=value2

We got the whole information over the URL when we used it in the place of the POST method, so this method is mainly used for retrieving the data.

- POST

It is used to send data to a server to create a resource. The data have sent to the server with POST request stored in the request body of the HTTP request:

- POST /test/demo_site.php HTTP/1.1

- Host: example.com

- name1=value1&name2=value2

CHAPTER SUMMARY

You have learned the basics of Django's template system with the concepts of tags and filters that exist both in Django's template language and in Jinja2. In the next chapter we will look at Django's admin panel.

## CHAPTER 7

Django's Admin Panel

IN THIS CHAPTER

➢ Overview of Django admin

➢ Django admin customization

➢ Custom layout

➢ Model admin classes

In the last chapter, we learned about Django templates, Jinja2, its syntax, and Django database with some python functions and inheritance. Here, we will learn about the admin panel of Django.

OVERVIEW OF DJANGO ADMIN

Django has an automatic admin interface. It reads all metadata from your models to provide a quick, model-centric interface where trusted users can manage content on your site. The admin's use is limited to an organization's internal management tool.

Django-admin.py is Django's command-line utility for administrative tasks management.

Usually, you will access Django-admin.py through a project's manage .py wrapper. manage.py is created automatically in each Django project and is a thin wrapper around Django-admin.py.

It takes care of two things for Django-admin.py:

DOI: 10.1201/9781003310495-7

- It puts your entire project's package on system path.

- It sets to the DJANGO_SETTINGS_MODULE environment variable into your project settings.py file.

ACCESSING THE DJANGO ADMIN SITE

When you ran the start project in the previous chapter, Django created and configured the default admin site. You need to create an admin user (superuser) to log in into the admin panel. Run the following command inside your virtual environment:

- python manage.py createsuperuser

Enter your desired username and press enter:

- Username

- (leave blank to use 'dell'): Quiz

- Error: That username is already taken.

- Username (leave blank to use 'dell'): quiz

- Email address:

- Password:

- Password (again):

- The username and password are too close.

- This is an insufficiently long password. It must be at least 8 characters long.

- Bypass password

- Validation and create user anyway? [y/N]: y

Superuser created successfully.

Now you have created an admin user, you are ready to use the Django admin. Let's run the development server and explore something new.

First, make sure the development server is running. Then open a web browser to http://127.0.0.1:8000/admin/. You should see the admin login screen.

Admin panel.

You may see the admin panel login window of Django in the above figure. Log in with the superuser account that you have created. Once logged in, you can see the Django admin page.

Admin panel.

You will see the admin panel of Django in the above figure. On the top of the page is the Authentication and Authorization group.

Groups and Users, both are provided by the authentication framework in Django.

Generally, when we are working on a single Django project, it's easier to use manage.py. If you want to switch between multiple Django settings files, use Django-admin.py with DJANGO_SETTINGS_MODULE or use the settings command-line option. The Django-admin.py script must be on your system path when you have installed Django via its setup.py utility. We will discuss it in brief subsequently (Django Admin Customization).

Enabling Admin Panel

The admin is allowed in the default Django project template used as start-project. If you do not want to use the default project template, here are the options:

- Add'django.contrib.admin' and its dependencies: django.contrib.auth, django.contrib.contenttypes, django.contrib.messages, and django.contrib.sessions. Add these codes into your setting.py in the place of INSTALLED_APPS.

- Configure the DjangoTemplates backend in your TEMPLATES setting using django.contrib.auth.context_processors.auth,django.template.context_processors.request, and django.contrib.messages.context_processors.messages in setting.py.

- The MIDDLEWARE setting, django.contrib.auth.middleware.Auth enticationMiddleware and django.contrib.messages.middleware.MessageMiddleware, must be included.

If you have to create an admin user to log in with, run the createsuperuser command in the terminal for the same project . By default, log in to the admin requires that the user details has the is_staff attribute set to True, otherwise you will not get access to your admin panel.

Application models must be changeable in the admin interface. For each of the models, register them with the admin, as described in ModelAdmin.

WHAT DOES ADMIN DO?

The admin let you register and write on any actions. Admin panel contains all the models you have created in your project. The basic workflow of Django admin is select an object, then change it, delete it, update it, and add it. Django admin tries to provide you a user interface for performing multiple operations (CRUD) on various user models with other functionalities like authentication, user access levels, etc. You will get to learn how the admin interface is customizable and how you can add and change the things in the admin. This modification may make it more productive.

HOW DOES IT WORK?

When Django loads your URLconf from urls.py at server startup, it executes the admin. This function iterates over your INSTALLED_APPS setting and looks for a file called admin.py in each installed app. In the admin.py in our books app, each call to admin.site.register() registers the given model. The admin site will display an edit/change interface only. The app django.contrib.auth includes its admin.py, which is why the Users and Groups showed up automatically in the admin. Other Django. contrib apps include Django.contrib. The Django admin site is just a Django application, with its models, templates, views, and URL patterns given with the admin.

HOW SECURE IS DJANGO ADMIN?

Django admin is handy at creating a database record to manage groups and users that give permissions to models at the level of reading, writing, modification, and according to what permission the user has. The Django admin itself is pretty safe. You can take additional measures by securing it via htaccess and force HTTPS access on it. The design is not responsive. Users on mobile devices need to do a lot of zooming and panning.

Writing Action Functions

First, we'll need to write a function called when the admin triggers the action. Action functions are regular functions that take three arguments:

- The current ModelAdmin

- An HttpRequest representing the current request

- A QuerySet containing the set of objects selected by the user.

Usage

Here are how to use django-admin.py:

- django-admin.py <subcommand> [options]

- manage.py <subcommand> [options]

It should be one of the subcommands listed in the "Available Subcommands", which is optional, should be zero, or more options available for the given subcommand.

Various Subcommands

- **Cleanup**: This can be run as a cron job or directly to clean out old data from the database (only expired sessions currently).

- **Compile messages**: The compile messages subcommand compiles .po files created, making messages to .mo files for use with built-in get text support.

- **createsuperuser**: This will create a superuser account (a user who has all permissions) that has full access to the site and requires permission using manage.py. It is useful if you need to create an initial superuser account. This command may be called in the terminal.

  The new account's username and e-mail address (optional) can be supplied by using the--username and --email arguments on the command line. This command is available only if Django's authentication system (Django.contrib.auth) is INSTALLED_APPS.

- **--locale**: use the --locale or -l option to specify the locale to process. If this option is not provided, all locales are processed.

- **Here is a usage example**: Django-admin.py compile messages --locale=br_PT

- **createcachetable**: This subcommand make a cache-table with a given name for use in the database-cache back-end.

- **Example**: django-admin.py createcachetable my_cache_table.

- **Runserver**: python manage.py runserver. You can run many servers as you want. Execute django-admin.py runserver more than once. To ensure your development server is clear to other machines on the web, run its default ip address (192.168.2.1) or 0.0.0.0 (which you can use if you don't know your IP address on the web).

  Some usage examples:

  o **django-admin.py runserver --adminmedia=/tmp/new-admin-stylefiles/**: Use the --admin media option to tell Django where to find the various CSS and JavaScript files for the Django admin interface.

  o **Django-admin.py runserver --noreload**: Use the --noreload option to disable the use of the auto-reloader.

Examples of using various ports and addresses:

o Port

o number is 8000:

o django-admin.py runserver

o IP address 127.0.0.1:

o django-admin.py runserver 7000

o 0.0.0.0:4000 (format is like this)

By default, the server does not serve any static files for your site (CSS, Images). All these have come under MEDIA_URL.

Django Admin Customization

Some portions of the Django Admin will be customized. This adjustment will allow us to see items in a more accurate manner.

Python manage.py Startapp Products

Install this application, type the product in the INSTALLED_APPS list in the settings.py file.

Now make models in the your app. The model will be used throughout this chapter to customize the Django admin.

```
from django.db import models
class Product_Details(models.Model):
  name = models.CharField(max_length = 200)
  description = models.TextField()
  def __str__(self):
    return self.name
```

We need to add this model into our admin panel and for that we need to migrate these changes to the database. Then, execute these commands in order in the same folder terminal. If you are using VS code, we will get it quickly. In the below screen, you can type these lines or with the command prompt, we need to open that folder in cmd (command prompt) and then run these commands.

```
python manage.py makemigrations
python manage.py migrate
```

These models must register in the Django admin. Edit the products/ admin.py file to accomplish this. After clearing the file, paste this code.

```
from django.contrib import admin
from .models import Product
# Register your models here.
admin.site.register(Product_Details)
```

In order to access the admin, we'll also need a superuser. If you already have a superuser account, you can relocate this section. Use this command to create a superuser in Django admin.

```
python manage.py createsuperuser
```

The password won't be displayed while you type for security purposes. After successfully creating a superuser, start your server.

```
python manage.py runserver
```

Now, we can start with Django admin. Paste this link into the browser: http://localhost:8000/admin/

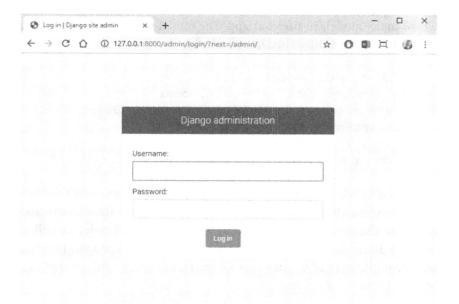

Admin panel.

How to Register/Unregister Models from Admin?
We can register models in the admin easily. We have to use the register method to register models in the admin. Also, we can unregister the model by the unregistering method.

```
admin.site.register(Product_Details)
admin.site.unregister(Group)
```

After unregistering the Group model, you will see that the Group model is not there.

Customization of Heading in Admin Panel
Add this line of code in your admin.py:
```
admin.site.site_header = "Django Practise"
```

Django Admin Custom Page Layout, Data, and Behaviors
There are multiple ways to customize the design, data, and behaviors of Django admin pages. You can customize specific global values used across all Django admin pages without the need to modify any Django template.

There are a number declarations on the admin. site object that is part of the Django.contrib package:

1. **admin.site.site_header**: It defines the title used beyond all Django admin pages (e.g., in the navy blue header and login page)

2. **admin.site.site_title**: It defines the title used. It defines all Django admin pages as part of the HTML title.

3. **admin.site.site_url**: It defines the domain (e.g., coffeehouse.com) to be used as part of the Django admin 'View site' link to access the live site from the Django admin easily.

4. **admin.site.index_title**: It defines the title of the main Django admin page.

5. **admin.empty_value_display**: It defines the default value to display when a Django admin model value is empty.

Model Admin Classes

It defines the representation of custom user-defined models in the admin panel. It is used to override various actions. There are many ranges of options opened with ModelAdmin Class.

ModelAdmin.exculde:

```
# ModelAdmin Class #
class Product_Deatils(admin.ModelAdmin):
  exclude = ('description', )
```

This ModelAdmin class overrides the default class views which the admin creates. In the above example, one of the variable 'descriptions' will be excluded. The exclude variable takes tuple; list as input or an array only name will be shown in the admin panel.

ModelAdmin.fields:

```
# ModelAdmin Class #
class Product_Deatils(admin.ModelAdmin):
  fields = ('name','description')
```

This model will change the layout of the model in the admin panel. The only fields shown are those which are defined in it.

ModelAdmin.fieldsts: Set the fieldsets to control the design and layout of admin "add" and "change" pages. fieldset is a list of two tuples, in which each two-tuple represents a <fieldset> on the form page. (A <fieldset> is small "section" of the Form.)

```
# ModelAdmin Class #
class Product_Deatils(admin.ModelAdmin):
  fields = ('name','description')
```

This model will change the layout of the model in the admin panel. The only fields shown are those which are defined in it.

```
class FlatPageAdmin(admin.ModelAdmin):
  fieldsets = (
    (Options, {
      'fields': ('url', 'title', 'content', 'sites')
    }),
    )
```

Fields can have the direct type of values in it as follows:

```
{
'fields': (('firstname', 'lastname'), 'address',
'city', 'state'),
}
```

ModelAdmin.form:

```
class CustomForm(forms.ModelForm):
  class Meta:
    model = Person
    exclude = ['name']
class Person_APanel(admin.ModelAdmin):
  exclude = ['age']
  form = CustomForm
```

In the above code, we create the dynamic form for our model to store values and define them in the AdminModel class.

ModelAdmin.list_display:

```
class PersonAdmin(admin.ModelAdmin):
  list_display = ('first_name', 'last_name')
```

Set list_display to control the fields that are displayed on the change list page of the admin.

1. **ModelAdmin.list_editable**: It will set list_editable to a list of field names on the model, which will allow editing on the change list page. It will be displayed as form widgets on the change list page, allowing users to edit and save multiple rows at once.

2. **ModelAdmin.list_filter**: To use this filter, define list_filter to activate filters in the sidebar of the list page of the admin. It might be a list or tuple of elements, where each piece should be one of the following types:

   1. The specified field should be either a BooleanField Type, CharField Type, DateField Type, DateTimeField Type, IntegerField Type, ForeignKey, or ManyToManyField Type

2. ModelAdmin.ordering:

   To use this filter, define set method to specify how lists of objects should be called in the Django admin views.

3. **ModelAdmin.paginator**: The paginator class is to be used for pagination. By default, Django.core.paginator.Paginator is used. Suppose the custom class does not have the same constructor interface. It will then also need to provide an implementation for ModelAdmin. get_paginator().

4. **ModelAdmin.radio_fields**: By default, Django admin uses a select-box interface (<select>) for selecting the fields that are ForeignKey or hold choices set. You have the option of using HORIZONTAL or VERTICAL from the Django.contrib.admin module.

5. **ModelAdmin.autocomplete_fields**: To use this filter, define autocomplete_fields as a list of ForeignKey and Many-To-ManyField fields if you would like to change to Select it to the autocomplete inputs.

6. **ModelAdmin.search_fields**: To use this filter, define set search_fields to allow a search box on the admin list page. It should be set to a list of field names that will be searched when somebody gives a search query in that text field box.

   These fields should be some text fields, such as CharField or TextField.

   Example,

   • search_fields = ['foreign_key__fieldname']

7. **class apps.AdminConfig**: It is default AppConfig class for the admin panel.

   autocover() will import an admin module in each application. Such modules are used to register model with the admin panel.

8. **Class apps.SimpleAdminConfig**: This class will work like AdminConfig, except it doesn't call autodiscover().

9. **ModelAdmin.date_hierarchy**: It is defined as set date_hierarchy to the name of a DateField/DateTimeField in your register model, and

the change list page will include a date-based drill down navigation by that field.

Example:

- date_hierarchy = 'date'.

10. **ModelAdmin.get_search_fields(request)**: This method is given the HttpRequest and return the same kind of kind type as for the search_fields attribute in the model.

11. **ModelAdmin.get_sortable_by(request)**: This method is passed the HttpRequest and is expected to return a collection (list, tuple, or sets) of fields that will be sorted in the change list page.

   Its default returns sortable_by if it set, otherwise it only defers to get_list_dispay().

12. **ModelAdmin.get_urls()**: This method of a ModelAdmin returns the URLs used for that ModelAdmin in the same way as a URLconf.

13. **ModelAdmin.get_form(request, obj, **kwargs)**: It returns a ModelForm class that is used in the admin panel to add and change views using see add_view() and change_view() methods.

   The base implementation is to subclass form, modified by attributes such as fields and exclude.

Some Permission Methods for AdminPanel

1. **ModelAdmin.has_view_permission(request, obj=None)**: It returns True if viewing obj is permitted, False otherwise. This class allows user read-only access to model when object is None, return True or False to indicate the way viewing of objects of this type is permitted.

   The default implementation is true if the user has only "view" permission.

2. **ModelAdmin.has_add_permission(request)**: It returns True if adding obj is permitted, False otherwise. This class allows user add-only access to model.

The default implementation is true if the user has only "add" permission.

3. **ModelAdmin.has_change_permission(request,   obj=None)**:It returns True if changing is permitted, False otherwise. This class allows user change-only access to model.

   The default implementation is true if the user has only "change" permission.

4. **ModelAdmin.has_delete_permission(request,   obj=None)**:   It returns True if the user obj has delete permission, False otherwise. This class allows user delete-only access to model.

   The default implementation is true if the user has only "delete" permission.

5. **ModelAdmin.response_add(request,   obj,   post_url_ continue=None)**: It is called after the admin form is submitted to the model and after the object. You can override the model to change the default behavior after the object has been created. It is used for adding new instance.

6. **ModelAdmin.response_change(request, obj)**: It is called after the admin form is submitted and after the object has been saved. It is used for changing the instance once.

7. **ModelAdmin.response_delete(request, obj_display, obj_id)**: It is called after the object has been deleted. It is used for delete instance once.

   obj_display: It is the first argument in a string with the name of the deleted object.

   obj_id: It is the first argument as the serialized identifier used to retrieve the object to be deleted.

8. **ModelAdmin.has_module_permission(request)**: It should return True if displaying the module on the admin index page and accessing the module's index page are permitted, False otherwise. Use User.has_module_perms() by default.

9. **ModelAdmin asset (Media and CSS)**: ModelAdmin has a feature of adding CSS, JavaScript, and Media in the Admin Panel.

```
from Django.contrib import admin
class CustomAdmin(admin.ModelAdmin):
 class Media:
  css = {
   'all': ('css/mymarkup.css',)
  }
  js = ('javascript/mymarkup.js',)
admin.site.register( CustomAdmin)
```

HOW TO ADD JQUERY IN YOU PROJECT?

Django allows us to use the jQuery library in the admin panel.

If you would like to use jQuery in your admin JavaScript without including a second copy, you can use the Django.jQuery object and add/edit views on the change list. Also, your admin forms or widgets depending on Django.jQuery must specify as follows:

```
from Django. contrib import admin.
class CustomAdmin(admin.ModelAdmin):
 class Media:
  css = {
   'all': ('css/mymarkup.css',)
  }
  js = ('admin/js/jquery.init.js',)
admin.site.register( CustomAdmin)
```

Adding custom validation to the admin: This Form consists of fields. Create a different file of name form.py, and then make a basic form structure and import it in admin.py.

Form.py looks as follows:

```
class CustomForm(forms.Form):
  name = forms.CharField(label='Your name',
max_length=100)
  age = forms.IntegerField(label='Your Age')
```

Here, the admin.py is needed to import that form for use directly in the admin panel.

```
from .form import *
class ArticleAdmin(admin.ModelAdmin):
  form = CustomForm
```

How to use form.py in view.py?

```
from .form import *
def register(request):
  # this is a POST request, need to process the form
data
  if request.method == 'POST':
    # create instance and populate it with data from
the request:
    form = NameForm(request.POST)
    # check whether it's valid:
    if form.is_valid():
      # process the data in form.cleaned_data as
required
      # ...
      # redirect to a new URL:
      return HttpResponseRedirect('/thanks/')
  # if a GET (or any other method) we'll create a
blank form
  else:
    form = CustomForm()
```

Let's understand each line of the code.

First, we import the CustomForm from form.py, and then we start our function named as register(). In the following line, we start our logic with if request.method, i.e., when the button is pressed, and its method is the same as "POST". Then the code written inside it will run, where we get the Form Data from the page form.py and store it in the form variable. We can call the Form is_valid() method; if it is not true, we can go back to the template with the Form. If is_valid() is True, we will be able to find all the validated form data in its cleaned_data attribute.

InlineModelAdmin: When two Django models share a foreign key relation, inline that can expose the related model on the parent model page is called InlineModelAdmin. It provides two subclasses of InlineModelAdmin:

1. TabularInline

2. StackedInline

InlineModelAdmin: It shares many of the same features as ModelAdmin, and adds some of its own. The shared features are as follows:

1. form

2. fieldsets

3. fields

4. formfield_overrides

5. exclude

6. filter_horizontal

7. filter_vertical

8. ordering

9. prepopulated_fields

10. get_fieldsets()

11. get_queryset()

12. radio_fields

13. readonly_fields

14. raw_id_fields

15. formfield_for_choice_field()

16. formfield_for_foreignkey()

17. formfield_for_manytomany()

18. has_module_permission()

InlineModelAdmin has its separate method:

- InlineModelAdmin.model:

  o **InlineModelAdmin.fk_name:** It is the name of the foreign key in the model. In few cases, this will be dealt with automatically, but fk_name must be specified explicitly if there will be more than one foreign key to the same parent model.

  o **InlineModelAdmin.formset:** This defaults to BaseInlineFormSet. Using your formset can give you many possibilities for alteration.

Inlines are built around model formsets.

- **InlineModelAdmin.form:** You cannot access any inline object inside any Inline Model. It is the only way to use a custom Modelform.

Examples

- self.instance.pk

- **InlineModelAdmin.get_extra():** It allows you to customize the number of different forms.

- **InlineModelAdmin.get_max_num():** It allows you to customize the maximum number of different forms.

- **InlineModelAdmin.get_min_num():** It allows you to customize the minimum number of displayed forms.

  1. **InlineModelAdmin.raw_id_fields ():** It is a list of fields you like to change into an input for either a ForeignKey or ManyToManyField as widget.

  2. **InlineModelAdmin.template:** This template used to render the inline model on the page.

  3. **InlineModelAdmin.verbose_name:** It is human-readable name in Django for the field. If it is not given, then Django can create it using the fields attribute.

     field_name = models. Field(verbose_name = "name")

  4. **InlineModelAdmin.has_add_permission(request, obj):** It should return True if adding a model object is permitted; False otherwise.

  5. **ys.:** We can do this with a foreign key, for example:

```
class Friendship(models.Model):
  to_person = models.ForeignKey(Student1, on_
delete=models.CASCADE, )
  from_person = models.ForeignKey(Student2, on_
delete=models.CASCADE,)
```

This can be done with the help of inline, and then there is no need to use a foreign key:

```
from Django.http import HttpResponseRedirect
from django.shortcuts import render
from Django.contrib import admin
from myapp.models import Friendship
class Friendships(admin.TabularInline):
  model = Friendship
  fk_name = "to_person"
class PersonAdmin(admin.ModelAdmin):
  inlines = [
    Friendships,
  ]
```

- **The Default Admin Site**: You can revoke the default django.contrib.admin.site by setting the default_site attribute of a custom AppConfig to the dotted import path of either an AdminSite subclass or a callable that returns a site instance.

- **Multiple admin sites in the same URLconf**: Create multiple instances of AdminSite and place each one at a different URL.

In this example, the URLs /basic/and/advanced/feature separate versions of the admin site – using the AdminSite instances myproject.admin .basic_site and myproject.admin.advanced_site, respectively:

```
# urls.py
from django.urls import path
from myproject.admin import advanced_site,
basic_site
urlpatterns = [
  path('basic/', basic_site.urls),
  path('advanced/', advanced_site.urls),
]
```

CHAPTER SUMMARY

In this chapter, we have learned about the admin panel and how it works, and how to register and unregister models. We also learned about ModelAdmin and its functions, and InlineModelAdmin and its functions. We will discuss Django's forms in the next chapter.

## CHAPTER 8

Django's Forms

IN THIS CHAPTER

➢ HTML forms

➢ Form classes

➢ Widget

➢ Looping over the form fields

➢ Django crisp forms

➢ User creation form

In the previous chapter, we learned about the admin panel, its working, register, and many functions. Here, we will discuss Django's most essential topic – Django forms.

HTML FORMS

They are used to take the input from the user in order to compile data. They are quite easy to use and handle all the validations for you. In HTML, the form is a collection of various elements inside <form>..other code..</form> that allow a user to do things like enter text, select options, manipulate objects or controls, add images, and so on, and then send that information back to the server. They also have various attributes like method, enctype, name, and so on. The <form> element might contain one or more element inside it:

DOI: 10.1201/9781003310495-8

- **<input>**: For entering text in the form

- **<textarea>**: For entering text like your message, feedback

- **<button>**: For submitting data to the server

- **<select>**: Used for dropdown list

- **<option>**: Should be written inside the <select>

- **<label>**: Used for defining the name

```
<form>
 <p>First Name: <input type="text"
name="firstname"></p>
 <p>Last Name: <input type="text"
name="lastname"></p>
 <p><input type="submit" value="Submit"></p>
</form>
```

Link to a Page with the Form

```
<a href="{% url 'post' %}" class="title"> You can
place text, image or anything else between the
anchor tag </a>
```

It is an HTML element that creates a link to target another URL. While implemented, the link can wrap-around text, images, or buttons so that users can interact with it and visit the link's destination.

An essential attribute of the <a> element is the href attribute, which indicates the link's destination. It has various attributes that should be written inside the anchor tags:

download	Target will be downloaded
href	Specifies the URL
rel	Set out the relationship between the current document and the other linked document
type	Specifies the media type of the linked document
target	_blank
	_parent
	_self
	_top, it states where to open the linked document

Input Tag

This <input> tag describes an input field where the user can enter data. It can be shown in various ways, depending on the type of attribute. The different input types are as follows: button, checkbox, color, date, email, number, password, submit, and file. These are the commonly used example.

```
<input type="text" class="form-control"
type="submit" name="username">
```

Django's Role in Forms

Django's form can simplify and automate a huge part of the work and do it more reliably than most programmers would be able to do in code. We can use it anywhere as it won't take much space. Django handles have three distinct parts:

- Preparing and restructuring data to make it ready for rendering to the user

- Creating HTML forms for the data

- Receiving and processing submitted forms and data from the client

Django's Forms

Django provides form classes that allow you to create HTML forms. It also describes a form and how it works and appears. Each field of the form class maps to the HTML form <input> element, and each is the class itself. It manages form data and performs validation while submitting the form.

```
from Django import forms
from .models import Post
#this is the forms
class CustomForm(forms.Form):
  first_name = forms.CharField(max_length=50)
  last_name= forms.CharField(max_length=50)
#this is the form that the model automatically
creates
class PostForm(forms.ModelForm):
  class Meta:
    model = Post
    fields = ('first_name', 'last_name',)
```

forms.Form vs forms.ModelForm

Two forms are created from forms. In ModelForm, we have to declare which model will be used to create our form.

First, we have to import Django forms (from Django import forms) and our ModelName model (from .models import ModelName). ModelNameForm, as you probably suspect, is the name of our custom form. It is necessary to tell Django that this form is a ModelForm – form. ModelForm is responsible for that. Next, we have class Meta (Meta provides you the information about the data) that tells Django which model should be used to create this form (model = ModelName). Finally, we add some fields in it like title and text.

'Form' refers to HTML <form> or Django form that provides structure to the form we can use it by import anywhere in any file. Every website has at least one form in it with which the user can interact.

The form has two essential state attributes:

1. **is_bound**: It will return False, and then it is an unbound state of form, that is, a new form with empty or default field values. If true, the form is bound; that is, at least one field has been set with user input.

2. **is_valid()**: If this returns true, every field in the bound form has valid data. If false, there was some invalid data in at least one field, or the form was not bound.

The Django Form Class

Form class describes a form that defines how it works and appears. For example, a ModelForm links a model class' fields to the HTML form <input> elements via a FormIt, which is represented to a user in the browser as an HTML 'widget'.

Bound and Unbound Form Instances

- **Unbound Form**: It is a form that has no data linked with it. When rendered to the user, it will be empty or will contain default values.

- **Abound Form**: It is a form that has submitted data and can be used to tell that data is valid. When an invalid bound form is rendered, it includes inline error messages telling the user what data to correct.

Widgets

It is Django's representation of an HTML input element. The widget handles all the rendering of the HTML.

```
from Django import forms
class CustomForm(forms.Form):
  title = forms.CharField(widget = forms.Textarea)
  description = forms.CharField(widget = forms.
CheckboxInput)
  views = forms.IntegerField(widget = forms.
TextInput)
  available = forms.BooleanField(widget = forms.
Textarea)
```

A widget is represented as an HTML input element. Django uses a default widget that is suitable to the type of data to be displayed. This would identify a form with a comment that uses a larger Textarea widget rather than the default TextInput widget.

The form class

```
from Django import forms
class NameForm(forms.Form):
  name = forms.CharField(label='Your name',
max_length=100)
```

Form rendering options:

- {{ **form.as_table** }}: It will render them as table cells wrapped in <tr> tags.

- {{ **form.as_p** }}: It will render them wrapped in <p> tags.

- {{ **form.as_ul** }}: It will render them wrapped in <li> tags.

Template	Code

{{ form.as_p }}	```html
	<div class="form" >
	<p>
	<label for="id_name"> Name:</label>
	<input class="textinput textInput formcontrol" id="id_name"
	 maxlength="100" name="name" type="text" />
	</p>
	<p>
	<label for="id_age">Age:</label>
	<input class="numberinput formcontrol" id="id_age" name="age"
	 type="number"/>
	</p>
	</div>
	``

{{ form.as_ul }}	```html
	<div class="form" >
	<li>
	<label for="id_name"> Name:</label>
	<input class="textinput textInput formcontrol" id="id_name"
	 maxlength="100" name="name" type="text" />
	</li>
	<li>
	<label for="id_age">Age:</label>
	<input class="numberinput formcontrol" id="id_age" name="age"
	 type="number"/>
	</li>
	</div>
	``

{{ form.as_table }}	```html
	<tr>
	<th>
	<label for="id_name">Name:</label>
	</th>
	<td>
	<input class="textinput textInput form-control" id="id_name"
	 maxlength="100" name="name" type="text" />
	</td>
	</tr>
	<tr>
	<th>
	<label for="id_number">Number:</label>
	</th>
	<td>
	<input class="textinput textInput form-control" id="id_number"
	 maxlength="100" name="number" type="number" />
	</td>
	</tr>
	``

There are various ways to show forms. Django forms help you create HTML representations of your forms. They support three separate representations: as_p (defined as paragraph tags), as_ul (defined as unordered list items), and as_table (as, unsurprisingly, a table).

Django defines a form class with a single field (name). The field maximum allowable length is defined by max_length. It puts a maxlength="150" on the HTML <input>. It also means that whenever Django receives the form back from the browser, it should validate the length of the data.

The Template: To add form in your template, you don't need to do much in the template:

```
<form action="/your-name/" method="post">
    {% csrf_token %}
    {{ form }}
    <input type="submit" value="Submit">
</form>
```

All the form's fields are fetched by {{form}} by Django's template language.

```
{% csrf_token %}
```

Cross-site Request Forgery (CSRF)protection: The CSRF's middleware and template tag protect against the CRSF attack. This type of attack occurs when various malicious website contains a link, a form button. How to use it? It should be activated by default in the MIDDLEWARE setting; remember that 'django.middleware.csrf.CsrfViewMiddleware'.

Widgets Argument

- **CharField() with Textarea widget attribute:**

```
from django import forms
# Create your forms here.
class ExampleForm(forms.Form):
    comment = forms.CharField(widget=forms.Textarea(at
trs={'rows':3}))
```

We can pass the various attributes in the widget for changes. Here we are changing the height with attributes in 'rows'.

- **DateField() with NumberInput widget attribute:**

```
from django import forms
from django.forms.widgets import NumberInput
# Create your forms here.
class ExampleForm(forms.Form):
  birth_date = forms.DateField(widget=NumberInput(
attrs={'type': 'date'}))
```

Here we separately import NumberInput at the top of the file and then add the NumberInput widget with the attribute 'type': 'date.' We can also add required as an additional parameter.

Various additional parameters

- Required

- max_length

- min_length

- label

- initial for CharField(), DateField(), BooleanField()

- **ChoiceField, MultipleChoiceField, ModelChoiceField, and ModelMultipleChoiceField:**

```
from Django import forms
# Create your forms here.
FAVORITE_COLORS = [
  ('blue', 'Blue'),
  ('green', 'Green'),
  ('black', 'Black'),
]
class ExampleForm(forms.Form):
  favorite_color = forms.ChoiceField(choices=FAVO
RITE_COLORS)
```

Use the Django ChoiceField as a string field for selecting a particular choice or to create a drop-down menu of choices. Each choice should have a key and a value. FAVORITE_COLORS are automatically fetched.

- **The Decorator Method**: Rather than adding CsrfViewMiddleware, you can use the csrf_protect decorator, which has the same functionality on particular views that need protection. But it has a security hole.

This is the basic structure of our new decorator:

```
import funct
ions
from Django. shortcuts import render
def view_form(form_cls, template):
  def decorator(func):
    @functools.wraps(func)
    def wrapper(request, *args, **kwargs):
      ...
    return wrapper
  return decorator
```

- **CSRF in Jinja2 Templates**: Django's Jinja2 template backend adds {{ csrf_input }} to the context of all templates which is equivalent to {% csrf_token %} in the Django template language. For example:

- <form method="post">{{ csrf_input }} or {% csrf_token%}</form>

- **Rendering Fields Manually**: You can get the data manually as per your needs. Suppose in the database you have fields name, age, marks, etc., and each field is available as an attribute of the form using {{ for.name_of_field }}:

```
<div class="wrapper">
  {{ form.message.errors }}
  <label for="{{ form.message.id_for_label }}">Your
message:</label>
  {{ form.name }}
</div>
<div class="wrapper">
  {{ form.message.errors }}
  <label for="{{ form.message.id_for_label }}">Your
message:</label>
  {{ form.age}}
</div>
<div class="wrapper">
  {{ form.message.errors }}
```

```
    <label for="{{ form.message.id_for_label }}">Your
message:</label>
   {{ form.marks}}
 </div>
```

- **Displaying Error**

- Using {{ form.name_of_field.errors }}: It displays a list of form errors, rendered as an unordered list. This might look as follows:

```
{% if form.subject.errors %}
 <ol>
 {% for error in form.subject.errors %}
   <li><strong>{{ error|escape }}</strong></li>
 {% endfor %}
 </ol>
{% endif %}
```

- **Looping over the Form's Fields**: Looping reduce the code by looping each field in turn using {% for %} loop:

```
{% for field in form %}
  <div class="wrapper">
    {{ field.errors }}
    {{ field.name }} {{ age }}
  </div>
{% endfor %}
```

Attributes of {{ field }}

- **{{ field.label }}**: It owns label attribute of the field, e.g., email name, address.

- **{{ field.label_tag }}**: It is the field's label attribute wrapped in the appropriate HTML <label> tag. This includes the form's label_suffix.

<label for="id_name">Name:</label>

- **{{ field.id_for_label }}**: The ID is used for this field.

- **{{ field. Value}}**: The value of the field. e.g., someone@example.com.

- **{{ field.html_name }}**: This will be the name of the field that will be used in the input elements like name field attribute. This only takes the form prefix into account if it has been set.

Syntax example,

- <input type="text" class="form-control"
- name="{{ form.name.html_name }}"
- id="{{ form.name.id_for_label }}" required>

- **{{ field.help_text }}**: The help text that has been associated with the field obtain the detailed information about that.

- **{{ field. Errors}}**: It contains any validation errors like syntax error corresponding to this field. You can then alert the user by displaying message. You can change the presentation of the errors occurring with a {% for error_name in the field. errors %} loop. In this case, the individual object in the loop is a string containing the error message.

Django-crispy-Forms

The Django-crispy-forms package makes writing the form template code more crispy. The new Django-uni-form was an application created by Daniel Greenfeld.

How to Use Django Crispy Forms

- pip install Django-crispy-forms in your Django project.
- Add crispy_forms to the list of installed apps in the settings.
- Add the crispy_template_pack to the settings.
- Load the Django crispy_forms_tags in the HTML template.
- Add the |crispy or |as_crispy_field filter to the Django form variable.

Example:

```
{% extends 'base.html' %}
{% load crispy_forms_tags %}
```

```
{% block content %}
<form method="POST">
{% csrf_token %}
{{ form_data |crispy }}
<button type="submit" class="btn btn-primary">Sign
in</button>
</form>
{% end block %}
```

Crispy Filter

It lets you render a form or formset using Django-crispy-forms elegantly div-based fields, and Django-crispy-forms implements a class called FormHelper, which defines the form behavior. The helpers give you a plan to control form attributes and their layout, and the |crispy filter has its built-in methods: as_table, as_ul, and as_p.

Installation

Install latest stable version Python environment using pip in the terminal:

```
pip install django-crispy-forms
```

Once the crispy form is installed using the above command, add the "crispy_forms" in INSTALLED_APPS in setting.py of the project.

```
INSTALLED_APPS = [
  'django.contrib.admin',
  'django.contrib.auth',
  'django.contrib.contenttypes',
  'django.contrib.sessions',
  'django.contrib.messages',
  'django.contrib.staticfiles',
  'crispy_forms' #add here
]
```

Application of crisp form:

1. A filter variable |crispy will render elegant div-based forms. It has the built-in methods: as_table; 2. as_ul; 3. as_p

   • The tag named {% crispy %} will render a form based on your configuration and specific layout. The below code will tell you that how you can add a crisp form to your template. Also, crispy forms use bootstrap classes by default, which affect this properly arranged, but simple layout.

```
{% load crispy_forms_tags %}
<h1>This Is My Crispy Form:</h1>
{% crispy form %}
```

Load in the Crispy Form Tags
The crispy form tags code will allow you to call the crispy form filters in the form below.

```
<html>
 <head>
   <!-- here adds meta tags -->
   <meta charset="utf-8">
   <meta name="viewport" ,initial-scale=1.0"conten
t="width=device-width, >
   <!--Bootstrap CSS-->
   <link href="https://stackpath.bootstrapcdn.com/
bootstrap/4.4.1/css/bootstrap.min.css" rel="style
sheet" integrity="sha384-Vkoo8x4CGsO3+Hhxv8T/Q5PaX
tkKtu6ug5TOeNV6gBiFeWPGFN9MuhOf23Q9Ifjh"
crossorigin="anonymous">
   </head>
   <body>
   {% load crispy_forms_tags %}
   <!--Contact form-->
   ...
   <!-- Optional Javascript -->
   <script src="https://code.jquery.com/jquery-3.4.1
.slim.min.js" integrity="sha384-J6qa4849blE2+poT4
WnyKhv5vZF5SrPo0iEjwBvKU7imGFAV0wwj1yYfoRSJoZ+n"
crossorigin="anonymous"></script>
   <script src="https://cdn.jsdelivr.net/npm/popper
.js@1.16.0/dist/umd/popper.min.js" integrity="sha3
84-Q6E9RHvbIyZFJoft+2mJbHaEWldlvI9IOYy5n3zV9zzTtmI
3UksdQRVvoxMfooAo" crossorigin="anonymous"></
script>
```

```
<script src="https://stackpath.bootstrapcdn.com/
bootstrap/4.4.1/js/bootstrap.min.js" integrity="sha3
84-wfSDF2E50Y2D1uUdj0O3uMBJnjuUD4Ih7YwaYd1iqfktj0U
od8GCEx13Og8ifwB6" crossorigin="anonymous"></
script>
  </body>
</html>
```

Using the Django as_crispy_field Form Filter

Use the format {{form.name_of_field|as_crispy_field}}. That way, you can change the order in which the form fields display.

```
<div>
  <h1>Contact</h1>
    <form method="post">
    {% csrf_token %}
    {{form.first_name|as_crispy_field}}
    {{form.last_name|as_crispy_field}}
      <button type="submit">Submit</button>
    </form>
</div>
```

WHAT TO DO WHEN THE CRISPY FORM IS NOT WORKING?

- Check that the installed package is named correctly.

- Make sure to add the crispy_template_pack to the settings.

- Be sure to load crispy_forms_tags at the top of the HTML template.

- The form filter used needs to either be |crispy or |as_crispy_field.

Template Packs

Django-crispy-forms: It has a built-in application that helps to manage forms in Django and it supports different CSS frameworks like Bootstrap, known as template packs within the Django-crispy-forms:

- Bootstrap is crispy-forms' default template pack, version 2 of the simple and flexible HTML, CSS, and JavaScript for user interfaces bootstrap3.

- Support for Twitter Bootstrap version 4.

- Uni-form is a nice-looking, well-structured, highly customizable, accessible, and usable form.

- This template pack is available through crispy-forms-foundation.

- Tailwind a utility first framework. This template pack is available through crispy-tailwind.

The crispy forms do not include static files like css and JavaScript. You will need to include the proper static and media files yourself, depending on what CSS framework (Template pack) you are using.

How to Style Django Forms with Bootstrap

Rendering a Django form with a Bootstrap requires you to pip install bootstrap4 or add the Bootstrap CDN and JavaScript to the file.
CDN

```
<!DOCTYPE html>
<html>
 <head>
   <!-- Required meta tags -->
   <meta charset="utf-8">
   <meta name="viewport" content="device-width,
initial-scale=1.0">
   <!--Bootstrap CSS-->
       <link rel="stylesheet" integrity="sha384-9a
It2nRpC12Uk9gS9baDl411NQApFmC26EwAOH8WgZl5MYYxFfc+
NcPbldKGj7Sk" href="https://stackpath.bootstrapcdn
.com/bootstrap/4.5.0/css/bootstrap.min.css"
crossorigin="anonymous">
 </head>
 <body>
<div class="container">
 <div class="row justify-content-center">
  <div class="col-8">
   <h1 class="mt-2">Django People</h1>
    <hr class="mt-0 mb-4">
     {% block content %}
     {% endblock %}
  </div>
 </div>
</div>
```

```
    <!-- Optional Javascript -->
    <script src="https://code.jquery.com/jquery-3.4.1
.slim.min.js" integrity="sha384-J6qa4849blE2+poT4
WnyKhv5vZF5SrPo0iEjwBvKU7imGFAV0wwj1yYfoRSJoZ+n"
crossorigin="anonymous"></script>
    <script src="https://cdn.jsdelivr.net/npm/popper
.js@1.16.0/dist/umd/popper.min.js" integrity="sha3
84-Q6E9RHvbIyZFJoft+2mJbHaEWldlvI9IOYy5n3zV9zzTtmI
3UksdQRVvoxMfooAo" crossorigin="anonymous"></
script>
    <script src="https://stackpath.bootstrapcdn.com/
bootstrap/4.4.1/js/bootstrap.min.js" integrity="sha3
84-wfSDF2E50Y2D1uUdj0O3uMBJnjuUD4Ih7YwaYd1iqfktj0U
od8GCExl3Og8ifwB6" crossorigin="anonymous"></
script>
    </body>
</html>
```

Form Helpers

The Django-crispy-forms app has a special class named FormHelper to make your life easier and give you enough power over how you want to render your forms.

Django UserCreationForm

The UserCreationForm is used to create a new user with built-in fields. Note that the user-created using "UserCreationForm" doesn't have email fields, so you can add it by adding more code of lines. It consists of the following primary attributes:

- username

- password

- first_name

- last_name

Implement Django UserCreationForm

To use the UserCreationForm, we need to import it from django.contrib .auth.forms.

```
from django.contrib.auth.forms import
UserCreationForm
```

Example of UserCreationForm:
form.py

```python
from django.shortcuts import render
from django.contrib.auth.forms import
UserCreationForm
# Create your views here.
 def register(request):
  if request.POST == 'POST':
    form = UserCreationForm()
    if form.is_valid():
      form.save()
  messages.success(request, 'Account created
successfully')
   else:
    form = UserCreationForm()
  context = {
    'form':form
  }
  return render(request, 'register.html', context)
```

register.html:

```html
  <div class = "register">
    {% if messages %}
    <ul>
      {% for message in messages %}
        <li>{{ message }}</li>
        {% endfor %}
    </ul>
  {% endif %}
        <form method="post" >
        {% csrf_token %}
        <table>
        {{ form.as_table }}
          <tr>
           <td></td>
           <td><input type="submit" name="submit"
value="Register" /></td>
        </tr>
        </table>
      </form>
    </div>
```

view.py:

```
from django.urls import path
from .views import *
  urlpatterns = [
  path('register', register, name = 'register')
]
```

After doing all the code, you just need to run the server and open this link in the browser, i.e., http://127.0.0.1:8000/register.

THE REASON WHY WE USE SELF.CLEANED_DATA

Data is passed as a string to the server, and even the browser gets everything as a string. When Django cleans the data, it automatically converts data to the appropriate type.

- name = form.cleaned_data['name']

Understanding Args and Kwargs in Python

Here, I will teach you what args and kwargs are, and how to use them.

What Are Args?

1. *args are used to pass non-keyword arguments. Examples of non-keyword arguments are fun(12,14), fun("value1","value2").

2. *args are usually used to prevent the program from crashing. If we do not know, numerous parameters will be passed to the function. This is used in other programming languages.

It makes it easy to use any number of arguments without having to change your code. It provides more flexibility to your code since you can have as many arguments as you wish in the future.

Example:

```
def func(*args):
  for arg in args:
    print(arg)
  func(11,22,33,"Django","Python")
list = [11,22,33,"Django","Python"]
func(list)
```

```
#OUTPUT
11
22
33
Django
Python
#List
[11, 22, 33, 'Django', 'Python']
```

What Are Kwargs?

**kwargs is a dictionary of keyword arguments. The double asterisk (**) symbol allows us to pass any number of arguments. A keyword argument is usually a dictionary.

Here an example of a keyword argument is fun(a=1,b=17).

**kwargs are similar to *args, except you declare the variables and the amount within the same function arguments.

Use of Args and Kwargs

Args and kwargs are handy when you need to:

- Pass multiple arguments in functions

- Reduce code writing

- Make your code more readable

- Reuse the piece of code

Using Both Args and Kwargs in a Function

When using both args and kwargs in the same function definition, *args must occur before **kwargs.

def __init__(self, *args, **kwargs):

CHAPTER SUMMARY

In this chapter, we covered HTML forms: how they work and their syntax. We also looked at implementing crisy forms with csrf_token, widgets and attributes in Django forms. We also learned about UserCreationForm. In the next chapter, we will learn about advanced models.

The Advanced Model

IN THIS CHAPTER

➢ Django's model definitions

➢ Fields

➢ Model method and objects

➢ User model

➢ Model manager

We looked at how web forms function in the last chapter and abstracted them using Django form classes. We also looked at how to save time while working with documents using various strategies and patterns.

In this chapter, we will discuss the advanced approach of Django Model code. We will dig much deeper into Django's models. We will cover adding and overriding model managers and model methods and how model inheritance works in Django.

DJANGO MODEL DEFINITION

Django's models are classes that provide an object-oriented way of dealing with databases. Each attribute corresponds to a database column, and each type belongs to a database table. An automatically produced API can be used to query these tables. It is usually defined in an application's model.py. They are applied as subclasses of Django.DB.models.Model and include fields, method, and metadata of class.

DOI: 10.1201/9781003310495-9

Models can serve as the foundation for a variety of other components. Once you've found a suitable model. Models are also employed in more locations than you would think. Django may be utilized in a number of ways:

```
from Django.DB import models
class ModelName(models.Model):
  # Fields of the model
s
  fieldname = models.CharField(max_length=50, help_
text='Enter field data')
  ...
  # Metadata
  class Meta:
    ordering = ['-fieldname']
  # Methods
  def get_absolute_url(self):
    return reverse('model-view', args=[str(self.id)])
  def __str__(self):
    return self.fieldname
```

Fields

A model can have a number of fields and each one represents a column of data to store the value in the model.

- **max_length=10:** It is stated that the maximum length of a value in this field is ten characters.

- **help_text=:** It just provides a text label to display value is to be entered by a user via an HTML form.

Common Field Arguments

The following common arguments can be used when declaring most of the different field types:

- **verbose_name:** It is a human-readable name for the field. If it is not specified, Django will infer the default verbose name from the field name.

- **Null:** Django will store blank values as NULL in the database for fields where this is appropriate if it is declared as true. The default is False.

- **Blank**: The field is allowed to be blank in your forms if it is True. The default is False, which means Django's form validation will allow you to enter a value. The null=True because if you allow blank values, you won't want to get them in the database to represent them appropriately.

- **Choices**: It is the sequence consisting of exactly two items ([(A.B)]). The first element in the such tuple is the name, and the second is iterable that contains a value.

- **primary_key**: It sets the current field as the primary key for the Model if it defines as true. (A primary key is a unique database column designated to identify all the different table records uniquely.) Django will automatically add a lot for this purpose if no field is specified as the primary key.

- **db_column**: This is the name of the database column to use as the field. Django will use the field's name if this isn't specified.

Fields for Common Data Types

- **CharField**: It is used to define short-to-mid-sized fixed-length strings. It specifies the max_length of the data to be stored.

- **TextField**: It is used for large length strings. You might specify a max_length for the field, and this is usually used in textarea.

- **IntegerField**: It is a field for storing integer (whole number) values.

- **DateField and DateTimeField**: hese are used for storing/representing dates and date/time information.

- **The E-mail field**: It is used to store and validate email addresses in the model.

- **FileField and ImageField**: These fields are used to upload files and images, respectively.

- **AutoField**: It is a special type of IntegerField that increments using primary key that automatically is added to your model if you don't manually specify.

- **ForeignKey**: It is used to specify a one-to-many relationship to another database model. The "one" refers to the relationship's model, which holds the "key" (models containing "foreign key" referring to "key" that are on "many" sides of such a relationship).

- **ManyToManyField**: This relationship is used to specify a many-to-many relationship.

Importing the model.py in Various Files

All package-level definitions must be defined in the global scope of __init__. py. For example, if we break models.py into distinct classes and store them in corresponding files such as p1.py, p2.py, and comment.py in the models subdirectory, the _init_ .py package would look like this:

- from p1.model import p1

- from p2.model import p2

Now you can import models as we have learned in the previous chapter.

Various Advanced Topics in Django Models

- **Automatic Primary Key**: The self.pk in the get_absolute_url() method occurs when this method is used. It returns as a reverse link to the URL, and this will pass an additional argument to the URL.

- **get_absolute_url ()**: It defines a get_absolute_url() method to tell Django how to calculate the URL for an object. To calls, this method should appear to return a string that can be used to refer to the object over HTTP.

- **String Representation**: When we printed out the list of students, all we got was this unhelpful display that makes it difficult to tell the student objects apart:

  o <QuerySet [<Student : Student object>, <Student : Student object>]>

  We can fix this by adding a method called __str__() to our student object. A __str__() method tells Python how to display an object's "string" representation. You can see in action by adding __str__() method.

```
class Student(models.Model):
    first_name = models.CharField(max_length=100)
```

```
last_name = models.CharField(max_length=100)
age = models.IntergerField(max_length=100)
def __str__(self):
  return self.first_name, self.last_name, self.age
#Run thses lines of code in the terminal.
>>> from books.models import Student
>>> Student_data= Student.objects.all()
>>> Student_data
<QuerySet [<Student:ABC>, <Student: XYZ>, <Student:
12>]>
```

- **Slug Field:** It is a field for storing URL slugs in a relational database. The slug field is similar to a char field but accepts fewer symbols by default: only letters, numbers, underscores, or hyphens. SlugField is defined within the Django.DB.models. Fields module is typically imported from Django.DB.models rather than including the fields module reference.

```
slug = models.SlugField(null=True, blank=True)
```

- **Meta Class**: This class allows us to define a lot more information on the whole collection of the item. Here, only the default ordering is set.

Model Method
Creating New Instances
To produce new instance of a model, For example:
  class Model(**kwargs):
The keyword arguments (kwargs) are the names of the fields you've defined on your model. To use your model, you just need to save that with save().

Customizing Model Loading
classmethod Model.from_db(db, field names, values)
This method can be used to customize your model instances when loading from the database.
  field_names.

Deleting Objects from Database
You can delete a field from a model instance, accessing it again and reload the value from the database. Example:

```
>>> obj = MyModel.objects.first()

>>> del obj.field

>>> obj.field # this code loads the field from the database
```

Model.get_deferred_fields()
A helper method returns a set containing the attribute names of all those fields that are currently deferred for this model.

Validating Objects
A validator is a callable that takes a value and raises a ValidationError if it doesn't meet some criteria.

Model.clean_fields(exclude=None)
This will be used to provide model modification and validation of your model.

```
class ModelName(models.Model):
    ...
    def clean(self):
```

Model.validate_unique(exclude=None)
This is similar to clean_fields() but validates all uniqueness constraints on your model. You can specify a list of field names to exclude from validation using the optional exclude parameter. If any fields fail validation, it will throw a ValidationError.

Saving Objects
To save an object to the database, call save():

```
Model.save(force_insert=False, force_update=False, using=DEFAULT_
DB_ALIAS, update_fields=None)
```

Auto-incrementing Primary Keys
An IntegerField automatically increments the available IDs. You usually do not need to use this directly.

Model.pk vs Model.id
Model.pk is the attribute that contains the value of the primary key for the model.

Model is the name of the field that was created as a primary key.

Model Objects
To construct an object, use the keyword parameters to the model class to instantiate it, then save() to store it to the database.

>>> from student import Student

>>> b = Student(name='ABC')

>>> b.save()

Behind the scenes, execute an INSERT SQL statement. There is no return value for save() function.

Saving ForeignKey and ManyToManyField Fields
Updating a ForeignKey field works the same way as saving a normal field. To create a relationship – an object that has a many-to-one relationship with itself – use models.ForeignKey('self', on_delete=models.CASCADE).

```
from Django.DB import models
class Car(models.Model):
  manufacturer = models.ForeignKey(
    'Manufacturer',
    on_delete=models.CASCADE,
  )
```

A many-to-many relationship occurs when various records in a table are associated with multiple records in another table.

```
From Django.DB import models
class Student(models.Model):
  name = models.CharField(max_length=30)
  def __str__(self):
    return self.name
class Examination(models.Model):
  subjects = models.CharField(max_length=100)
  student_record = models.ManyToManyField(Student)
  def __str__(self):
    return self.subjects
```

save() and add()

save(), Django will save the current object state to record. and add() include multiple argument in the call to add(), like this:

>>>riya= Student.objects.create(name="Riya")

>>>george = Author.objects.create(name="George")

>>>ringo = Author.objects.create(name="Ringo")

>>>model.Student..add(john, paul, george, ringo)

Retrieving All Objects
details = Student.objects.all()
The all() method returns a Query Set of all the objects in the database. Django has so many methods that return Query Sets.

Method	Description
filter()	Filter by the given lookup parameters
1.exclude()	Filter by objects that don't match the given lookup parameters
2.annotate()	Annotate each object in the QuerySet. Annotations can be simple values, a field reference, or an aggregate expression
order_by()	Change the default ordering of the QuerySet
reverse()	Reverse the default ordering of the QuerySet
distinct()	Perform an SQL SELECT DISTINCT query to eliminate duplicate rows
values()	Returns dictionaries instead of model instances
values_list()	Returns tuples instead of model instances
dates()	Returns a QuerySet containing all available dates in the specified date range
datetimes()	Returns a QuerySet containing all available dates in the specified date and time range
none()	Create an empty QuerySet
all()	Return a copy of the current QuerySet
union()	Use the SQL UNION operator to combine two or more QuerySets
intersection()	Use the SQL INTERSECT operator to return the shared elements of two or more QuerySets

difference()	Use the SQL EXCEPT operator to return elements in the first QuerySet that are not in the others
select_related()	Select all related data when executing the query (except many-to-many relationships)
AND -	It will combine two QuerySets with the SQL AND operator. Its symbol is (&) operator. Its functionality is equivalent to filter() with multiple parameters
OR :	It will combine two QuerySets with the SQL OR operator. Its symbol is (|) operator

prefetch_related()	It selects all related data when executing the query. It is designed to stop the deluge of the database. It makes a separate loop for each relationship
defer()	It will retrieve the named fields list of fields_name from the database. It is used to improve query performance on complex datasets
only()	() – return only the named fields
Opposite of defusing()	Select which database the QuerySet will be evaluated against (when using multiple databases)
select_for_update()	Return a QuerySet and lock table rows until the end of the transaction
raw()	Execute a raw SQL statement

Other model instance methods

Model.__str__() The __str__() method represents our QuerySet text in human-readable form. It is defined in a way that is easy to read. This method is also used as a debugging tool when the class members need to be checked.

```
from Django.DB import models
class Person(models.Model):
  first_name = models.CharField(max_length=50)
  last_name = models.CharField(max_length=50)
  def __str__(self):
    return self.first_name, self.last_name
```

Model.__eq__(): This method of a class is used when you use the == operator to compare the instances of the class.

```
class Student:
  def __init__(self, firstname, lastname, age):
    self.firstname = firstname
```

```
  self.lastname = lastname
  self.age = age
def __eq__(self, other):
  return self.age == other.age
```

UserModel

The default User model in Django uses a username to identify a user during authentication uniquely. It has the following:

- User

```
from django.db import models
from django.contrib.auth.models import User
# Create your models here.
class Student(models.Model):
  author = models.ForeignKey(User, on_
delete=models.CASCADE)
  name = models.CharField(max_length=50)
  def __str__(self):
    return self.name
```

AUTH_USER_MODEL: It is the recommended approach when referring to a user model in a models.py file.

For this, you need to create a custom User Model by subclassing.

1. **AbstractUser**: It is a complete User Model with fields as an abstract class so that you can inherit data from it and add your profile fields and methods.

2. **AbstractBaseUser**: It only contains the authentication functionality. You can import both using django.contrib.auth.models import AbstractUser, AbstractBaseUser

3. **User model:**

```
from django.db import models
from django.contrib.auth.models import User
# Create your models here.
class Student(models.Model):
  marks= models.ForeignKey(settings.AUTH_USER_MOD
EL, on_delete=models.CASCADE)
```

```
name = models.CharField(max_length=50)
def __str__(self):
  return self.name
```

- Get_user_model()

```
from django.db import models
from django.contrib.auth import get_user_model
User=get_user_model()
# Create your models here.
class Student(models.Model):
  author = models.ForeignKey(User, on_
delete=models.CASCADE)
  name = models.CharField(max_length=50)
  def __str__(self):
    return self.name
```

Here we pass get_user_model in some variables to use that in the following statement.

User Model Built-in Fields

Username: Required 50 characters or fewer. Usernames may contain alphanumeric, _, @, +, ., and - some special characters.

- **first_name**: This allows us to add the first name with various fields like blank=True, null.

- **last_name**: This allows us to add the last name with various fields like blank=True, null.

- **Email**: This allows us to add emails with various fields like blank=True, null.

- **Password**: Django doesn't store the raw password for this. You have to set the encrypted password.

- **groups**: Used for many-to-many relationships.

- **is_staff**: Designates whether this user can access the admin site.

- **is_active**: Designates whether this user account should be considered active when the user is logged in.

- **is_superuser**: User permission for handling the admin stuff.

- **last_login**: A date–time of the user's last login.

- **date_joined**: A DateTime identified when the account was created.

- **is_anonymous**

- **is_authenticated**

Methods

- **get_username()**: It returns the username for the user.

- **get_short_name()**: It returns the first_name plus the last_name, with a space in between.

- **get_full_name()**: It returns the first_name of the user.

- **set_password(raw_password)**: It sets the user password to the provided raw string, and then uses this method to encrypt the password. When the raw_password is nothing, the password will be set to an unusable password, and then set_unusable_password() is used.

- **check_password(raw_password)**: Returns True if the given raw string is the correct password for the user.

- **set_unusable()**: It marks that the user having no password.set.check _password() for this user will never return True. Doesn't save the user object.

- **Authenticate (request, username)**: The username passed as the username is considered. This method returns back the user object with the provided username, c.

Logout and Login Signals

- **user_logged_in()**: It returns when a user logs in successfully.

Various arguments sent with some signal:

  o **Sender**: The user class that just logged in to the model.

  o **Request**: It sets the current HttpRequest instance for the class.

- o **User**: The user that just logged in.

- **user_logged_out()**: It is sent when the logout method is called.

  - o **Sender**: The user that just logged out or none if the user was not authenticated.

  - o **Request**: It returns the current HttpRequest object.

  - o **User**: The user object that just logged out.

Manager Methods

create_user(username, email, password, **extra_fields): The username and password are set as given. The email is converted to lowercase, and then the returned user object will have is_active set to True, and when no password is provided, set_unusable_password() will be called. The extra_fields keyword arguments are passed through to the User's __init__ method to set arbitrary fields on a custom user model.

create_superuser(username, email=None, password=None, **extra_fields): Same as create_user() with its attributes.

Model Manager

A Manager is a Django class that provides the interface between database query operations and a Django model. The manager is the interface that interacts with the database.

A Custom Name to the Default Manager

There is a need to give a custom name to your default manager. You have to define a class attribute or field in the model of type models.Manager(). Here is an example:

```
class Student(models.Model):
  students = models.Manager() #now the default
manager is named as students
```

How to Use the Student Manager

Student.students.filter() // here students manager is used.

Methods of Manager Class

Method Class	Description
all()	It returns a query set containing all objects created so far
filter(**kwargs)	It returns a query set containing a list of objects that match with the given arguments. If no matched thing is found, it returns an empty query set
exclude(**kwargs)	It does precisely the opposite of the filter() method, i.e., returns a queryset containing objects that do not match with given arguments
get(**kwargs)	It returns a single object that matches the given argument. If multiple objects are found, it will throw a Model. MultipleObjectsReturned error. If get() doesn't find any object, it raises a model – there does not exist exception
create(**kwargs)	It creates a new object with given arguments
order_by(*fields)	It sets the ordering of the previously returned queryset according to the arguments passed in it

CHAPTER SUMMARY

In this chapter, we learned about Django's model with its types of methods. We also learned about the standard model methods, which return some kind of QuerySets, model field lookups, aggregate functions, and build complex queries. We also covered adding, overriding model managers, model methods, and how model inheritance works in Django.

Deployment

IN THIS CHAPTER

➢ Introduction to deployment

➢ Choosing right hosting providers

➢ Deployment with AWS

➢ Deployment with Microsoft Azure

➢ Deployment wit Git

The previous chapter discussed the advanced model and various methods of models with coding examples. Here, in this chapter, we will discuss how to deploy the Django project over the internet.

INTRODUCTION

Django is a robust Python-based web framework that allows you to deploy your applications or websites over the internet. Django may include many features such as authentication, a custom database ORM (object-relational mapper), and an expandable plugin architecture using third-party websites. It simplifies the complexities of web development, allowing you to focus on writing code.

Prerequisites

Python 3 needs to be installed on your local machine. You can follow installation steps from Chapter 2 (for Windows, LINUX/UNIX, macOS).

DOI: 10.1201/9781003310495-10

There are other various steps to follow:

Step 1 is the creation of the Python Virtual Environment for the project.

Before you get started, you need to set up our Python developer environment. You will install your Python requirement within a virtual environment to make things easy.

What Is a Deployment Environment?

It is a shortcut to making your website live. This will change the only way to deliver your product code to the client. The environment includes:

- Computer hardware on which the website runs.

- Your Operating system (e.g., Linux, Windows).

- Programming language runtime and framework libraries in which your website is written.

- The web server is used to serve pages and other content (e.g., Nginx, Apache).

- An application server that passes "dynamic" requests between your Django website and the webserver.

- Databases on which your website is dependent.

PYTHON INSTALLATION ON WINDOWS

Now, here is the step to install Python in your system.

Download the latest Python 3 (64-bit) installer from the official Python website, usually Windows x86-64 MSI installer. The SDK does not support the 32-bit Python interpreter.

1. **Click on the Install Now**

   Installation path: I

   You have to check that check box that says "Add Python 3. x to Path", as shown below the Install launcher for all users.

2. **Installation in Process**

   It will take some time because all the in-built functions, modules, and packages are installed.

3. **Installation complete**

Now the installation is completed.

Now, run the Python command on the command prompt. Type the command Python version in case of python3 or Python.

Now next step is to add Python PATH to the environment variable.

How to Add PATH in Environment Variable

1. Search Environment in your search bar.

2. The Window pops up and will show edit the system environment variable.

3. Then in the first shell, you will see the PATH open it and add the NEW path in it.

When you run the Python command in your shell or command prompt, the Python interactive session begins. You can perform your code here.

- C:\Users\PC>python3

- Python 3.9.7 (tags/v3.9.7:1016ef3, Aug 30 2021, 20:19:38) [MSC v.1929 64 bit (AMD64)] on win32

- Type "copyright", "help ", "credits", or "license" for more information.

INSTALLING DJANGO WITH PIP

Before installing Django, install the virtual environment setup with the help of pip commands as mentioned above. The virtual environment is used to execute the Django application and it is a package in Python called virtualenv for a different project, and we install it from the command line using pip:

- pip install virtualenv

- Make sure your pip version is up to date. You can do it this way.

  Pip install – upgrade pip.

- You require to create a virtual environment for your

  project by writing:

  Virtual environment setup with pip

  virtualenv your_enviornment_name

  Or

  python3 –m venv your_enviornment_name (You can give any name to your environment)

Next, confirm the environment (name can be anything) directory has been created by listing all the guides using the ls command:

- >ls

Once your virtualenv has finished setting up your new virtual environment, open
Windows Explorer and have a look at what virtualenv created for you. In your
root directory, you will now see a folder called \ your_enviornment_name (or whatever name you gave to the virtual environment). Open your project folder, and then you will see the following:

- C:\Users\PC\Desktop\Python-Project\env\Scripts
- (env is your environment name).

To use this new Python virtual environment, we have to activate it, so let's go back to the command prompt and type the following:

- Activating the Virtual Environment
- your_enviornment_name/Scripts/activate

This will run the activate Script inside your virtual environment's \Scripts folder. You will notice your command prompt has now changed:

- (env) C:\Users\PC\Desktop\Python-Project\env\Scripts

- Now your Python virtual environment is working. Let's install Django in it.

Creation of the Django Project

Create a project using the Django-admin tool that was installed when you installed Django:

- django-admin startproject app_name

Then your current directory will contain the following content:

manage.py: A Django project management script.

django_app/ allows you to interact with the Django project. It is the core of the Django project. It should contain the __init__.py, settings.py, urls.py, asgi.py, and wsgi.py files.

These files will be the root directory of your project. Then navigate into this directory with the command: run this command in the terminal:

- cd app_name

CHOOSING THE RIGHT HOSTING PROVIDER

Many hosting providers support Django or work well with deploying.

Various factors need to consider when choosing a host.

- Understand the needs of your site

The very first step towards choosing the right web host is to identify your needs for your website. Ask questions such as, "What type of website should I build the building?" If you are a complete beginner, then go and share your plan with a trusted company.

The potential to upgrade your hosting server plans come in various shapes and sizes today. But if you're just starting, lookout for web hosts that offer the flexibility and extension to scale up when your website demands it if you're a beginner.

- Do they have the essential features?

Every time you should check if they offer other essential features such as a file manager, one-click installer, and DNS management.

1. **One-click installer**

   This type of installer is a great tool to help you straightforwardly install the high-level configuration:

   high range of popular applications WordPress, Drupal, Joomla, etc.

2. **.htaccess File Access**

   It is a powerful website that looks over the file.

   If you wish to make site-wise administrative changes, you will have to access the .htaccess file. It also provides a way to make changes to a directory.

3. **FTP/SFTP access**

Many hosting providers will offer some form of file manager, which tends to be quite limited. With FTP/SFTP access, you will safely handle and move large amounts of files on the server.

- Having backups for your site in local drive or over the cloud helps you a lot more.

They are essential for a website. Even with all the safety measures globally, your website will face several kinds of viruses, crashes, failures, or hacks that will lay your website down fully.

It can create a copy of your project on their sever, so whenever any incident happen you can get from your backup.

- **Capacity for long-term growth:** A web host will have all the essential resources that you need to grow your company up. Your host should offer you every hosting to help you to progress from small to large.

Ready to Publish Your Website

The Django website is created using the Django-admin, and manage.py tools are figured out to make development easier. Many of the Django project settings are specified in settings.py that should be different for production, either for security or performance reasons.

Some mandatory settings that you need to check are as follows:

- **DEBUG**: It should be put False in production (DEBUG = False), then this will stop the delicate/sensitive debug trace and variable information from being displayed.

- **SECRET_KEY**: This is a considerable random value used for CSRF protection etc. The key used in production is in Django. When we run Django-admin startproject, it automatically adds a randomly generated SECRET_KEY to every new project.

- **ALLOWED_HOSTS:** It needs to be set to an allowlist of the IP addresses/domain names that your app can use to prevent cross-site request forgery attacks or something like that.

- **DATABASES**: Database connection parameters are probably different in development and production. Database passwords are susceptible. It would be good if you protect them exactly like SECRET_KEY. For maximum security, make sure database servers only accept connections from your application servers.

DJANGO DEPLOYMENT INTERFACES

There are various options for deploying your Django project application based on your pattern or particular business needs.

Django, being a web framework, needs a web server to operate. And since most web servers don't natively speak Python, we need an interface to make that communication happen.

Django currently supports two interfaces: WSGI and ASGI.

These two files are located inside the project.

WSGI

WSGI is the leading Python standard for communication between web servers and applications, but it only supports synchronous code. WSGI is the Web Server Gateway Interface. It describes how a webserver executes the web app and sends the information to the client. It plays an indispensable role at the time when you deploy your Django or Flask Application.

Why is it necessary?

It is servers that are designed to handle so many requests concurrently. All frameworks are not made to process thousands of submissions. That's why we use it to speed up your Python web application development because you only need to know basic things about WSGI.

Preparing our WSGI server:

The WSGI blueprint makes it so that any WSGI compatible web server can run any WSGI consistent web framework, which means:

- Green Unicorn (Gunicorn) is a pre-fork worker model-based server ported from the Ruby Unicorn project. It is a Python WSGI server for the UNIX system. It is based on an a-fork model compared to a worker model architecture.

```
python -m pip install gunicorn
```

When Gunicorn is installed, a gunicorn command is available, which starts the Gunicorn server process.

```
gunicorn myproject. WSGI
```

- uWSGI is gaining steam as a highly performance WSGI server implementation.

  uWSGI operates on a client-server model. Your web server (e.g., Nginx, Apache) communicates with a Django-uwsgi "worker" process to serve dynamic content.

- mod_wsgi is an Apache module implementing the WSGI specification.

  mod_wsgi is an Apache HTTP Server module for Python-based host any Python2. It is an alternative to mod_python, FastCGI solutions.

  Basic files structure:

```
WSGIScriptAlias / /path/to/mysite.com/mysite/wsgi.py
WSGIPythonHome /path/to/venv
WSGIPythonPath /path/to/mysite.com
<Directory /path/to/mysite.com/mysite>
<Files wsgi.py>
Require all granted
</Files>
</Directory>
```

- CherryPy is a pure Python web server that also functions as a WSGI server. It has built-in tools for sessions, static files, cookies, file uploads, caching, encoding, authorization, compression, and many more.

Here are some WSGI compatible web frameworks:

- Django

- Flask

- Pyramid

- web2py

Configuring the settings module:
When the WSGI server loads your application, Django needs to import the settings module. Django uses the DJANGO_SETTINGS_MODULE environment variable to locate, for example,

- os.environ["DJANGO_SETTINGS_MODULE"] = "my site.settings

Applying WSGI Middleware:
A WSGI Middleware component is a Python callable.

ASGI

ASGI is the new, asynchronous-friendly standard that will allow your Django site to use asynchronous Python features and asynchronous Django features as they are developed. The Asynchronous Server Gateway Interface (ASGI) is the specification for extending the capabilities of WSGI (Web Server Gateway Interface).

This Application is a callable that takes scope and returns a coroutine callable that receives and send methods. It is usually written as a class:

class Application
    def __init__(self, scope):
    async def __call__(self, receive, send):
    The scope holds the properties of a connection.
    It has two interfaces:
    In the async syntax method, we have __call__method, which makes it an actual point of task-switchers with others, and allows other code (asynchronous code) to be used with that execution context.

The second interface receives and sends arguments, over which the messaging occurs between the server and Application. The receive available provides events as dicts as they occur, and the send av.

AWS?

The full form of AWS is Amazon Web Services. It offers Amazon a more flexible, reliable, scalable, easy-to-use, and cost-effective cloud computing solutions platform. This platform provides you the combination of Desktop as a Service (DaaS), Platform as a Service (PaaS), and Software as a Service (SaaS). It is the most comprehensive and broadly adopted cloud platform.

What Is Cloud Computing?

Cloud computing means storing, accessing data, and programs over the Internet. It is an application-based software infrastructure that stores data on small serves, accessed through the Internet.

Types of Clouds

There are three types of cloud:

1. **Public cloud**: In this cloud, the third-party service providers make all the resources and services available to their customers via the internet.

2. **Private cloud**: A private cloud has almost the same feature as the public, but all the organizations manage all the resources. The main work to focus on is infrastructure.

3. **Hybrid cloud**: A hybrid cloud is a combination of both private and public clouds. Its strategy provides you the greater flexibility in your businesses. It helps organizations replicate on-premise workloads and backup over the cloud server.

Cloud Services Models

- **IaaS:** It stands for Infrastructure as a Service. It provides users with the capability to process, storage, and network connectivity on demand.

- **PaaS:** It stands for Platform as a Service. This will provide services like databases, queues, workflow, and the engine, which has resources to focus more on their Application's functionality.

AWS SERVICES

It (Amazon Web services) offers a wide range of business, primarily cloud-based products. The products must include storage, database, analytics, network, various development tools, and many more. Now, let's talk about the AWS Compute Services provided by Amazon.

It has been a building block for those organizations as they are used for creating and developing any Application over the cloud. Various domains of Amazon Web Services are Compute, Storage, Database, Migration, Network, Content Delivery, Management Tools, and Security and Identity Compliance.

There are various best services offered by AWS:

1. **Amazon Elastic Cloud Compute (EC2)**: It provides services that assist compute workloads, and its web interface is used to reduce the expensive physical servers by creating virtual machines. Amazon EC2 is preferable while creating a virtual server within a few minutes with just a few clicks according to the user's operating system. This helps a lot to focus more on the project rather than the server maintenance.

2. **Amazon S3 (Simple Storage Service)**: This domain provides data storage over internet services. It stores the data with high security because of its improved infrastructure. The information is distributed over different regions and has high-quality integration. It blocks the data from getting lost and helps retrieve stored time and space data via the internet.

3. **Amazon Virtual Private Cloud (VPC)**: It falls under the networking domain of AWS used to isolate the network infrastructure of one's computer. It holds a unique virtual network that protects the information from others and makes the user information risk-free in the cloud.

4. **Amazon Cloud Front**: It represents the delivery domain that is used to deliver the content with good speed and reduce latency. It effectively manages all the user content via the Global Content Delivery Services.

AWS ELASTIC BEANSTALK

It is an easy-to-use service for deploying and scaling web applications and services developed with Python, Ruby, and Go. You can automatically upload your code into Elastic Beanstalk that handles the Application's deployment, load balancing, and autoscaling. There are no additional charges for Elastic Beanstalk.

Benefits

- **Fast and straightforward**: It is the quickest way to deploy your application on AWS. You use the AWS management console, a Git repository, or IDEs suck as Visual Studio to upload your whole project.

- **Developer productivity**: It manages the Application's infrastructure. It will keep the underlying platform running your Application up to date with the latest features.

- **Complete resource control**: It allows retaining full control over the AWS resources powering your application. You can select any AWS resources such as AC2 that will provide optimally for your Application.

Now create the virtual environment to use the ASW services.

First, sign up and have an ASW account and login credentials. To learn more about it, visit https://aws.amazon.com/

It would be best if you had all of the Common Prerequisites for Python installed, including the following packages:

- Python 3.7 or later

- pip

- virtual

- awsebcli

Our requirement for Django is done. Now configure your Django application for Elastic Beanstalk.

By default, Elastic Beanstalk has a file named application.py to run their Django application. Because this does not exist in the Django project that you have created, you need to make something to set your application environment. You must also keep the environment variables so that your Application's modules can be loaded.

To configure your site for Elastic beanstalk, activate your site for Elastic Beanstalk.

In Unix-based system following this command, open your project folder and activate it:

- C:\Users\PC\Django_project> virtual\Scripts\activate.

Run pip freeze in the terminal, and then save the output to a file named requirement.txt (here you will get the list of every installed package in your project):

- Pip freeze >requirement.txt

- Create a Directory named .ebextensions, using this command

- mkdir extensions

- In the .ebextensions directory/folder, add a file named as djnago.conf ig with the following:

- Example :/ebdjango/.ebextensions/django.config

- option_settings:

- aws:elasticbeanstalk:container:python:

- WSGIPath: ebdjango.wsgi:application

WSGI path will specify the location of the WSGI script that Elastic Beanstalk uses to start your Application.

To deactivate your virtual environment with the deactivate command,

- >>> deactivate

Reactivate your virtual environment whenever you need to add packages to your Application or run your Application locally.

- **Design your new Application in the AWS EB CLI**

In Windows,

```
Enter Application Name
(default is "my site"): Django-deployment
Application Django-deployment has been created
```

In macOS terminal,

```
Enter Application Name
(default is "my site"): Django-deployment
Application Django-deployment has been created
```

AWS CLI asks for an application name, and your application name is Django-deployment. Multiple environments can be within one Application. AWS Elastic Beanstalk is comprised of Application and environment. Before telling your application name, enter your credentials.

- **Your preferable programming language**

In the macOS terminal,

```
It appears you are using Python. Is this correct?
(Y/n): y
Select a platform version.
1) Python 3.6
2) Python 3.4
3) Python 3.4 (Preconfigured - Docker)
4) Python 2.7
5) Python
(default is 1): 1
```

Windows Command Prompt:

```
It appears you are using Python. Is this correct?
(Y/n): y
Select a platform version.
1) Python 3.6
2) Python 3.4
3) Python 3.4 (Preconfigured - Docker)
4) Python 2.7
5) Python
(default is 1): 1
```

The CLI knows which programming language you are using. To respond, type y, and then select the latest version of Python.

- **Configure SSH security connection**

SSH (Secure Socket Shell) is a secure connection allowing the developers to access a server remotely. This connection enables the user to safely access system administration and transfer files without fearing an insecure network connection.

When connecting to a host via SSH, SSH key pairs are often used to authorize users individually. These organizations are responsible for storing, sharing, managing access for, and maintaining these SHH keys.

In Window and macOS, the output will be as follows:

```
Do you want to set up an SSH key for your instances?
Object?
(Y/n): y (y if yes you want to set up )
Select a keypair.
1) aws-eb
2) [ Create new KeyPair ]
(default is 1): 1
```

- **Now create the environment for your project**

macOS:

```
eb create Django-env
```

Windows Command Prompt:

```
C:\Users\PC> eb create Django-env
```

Run the command create Django-env to create a new environment named Django-env (this can be anything). The environment will reset and begin to configure by itself based on the files we added before the project automatically.

- **Check the status of the environment**

macOS terminal:

```
Facebook-user: site user$ eb status
Environment details for Django-env
 Application name: Django-deployment
```

```
. . .
CNAME: django-env......elasticbeanstalk.com
```

In Windows Prompt:

```
C:\Users\PC> eb status
Environment details for: django-env
 Application name: django- deployment
 . . .
 CNAME: Django -env......elasticbeanstalk.com
```

Check the status of the environment after it has been perfectly installed in your system. The Elastic Beanstalk (EB) domain AWS has been automatically created for your application. CNAME value is the Elastic Beanstalk domain name of your website.

- **Add your custom EB domain name to setting.py**

```
ALLOWED_HOSTS = [
  'django-env.........elasticbeanstalk.com'
]
```

Go to your setting.py of your Django project; add the above line of code of CNAME in ALLOWED_HOSTS. Place all the tests in between quotations (' ').

- **Replace the Django DEBUG settings in the .env file**

```
DEBUG = True
```

We have left DEBUG =TRUE until we can still receive a yellow Django page whenever any error occurs. But in the deployment, we do not want users to get the debug page if they type in a nonexistent URL; they should get a 404 error instead. Turn the DEBUG to False and save the changes.

```
DEBUG = False
```

- **Upload the project to AWS Elastic Beanstalk**

In macOS:

```
Macbook-user:site user$ eb status
Environment details for: django-env
```

```
Application name: django-deployment
...
Status: Ready
Health: Green
User-Macbook: my site user$ eb deploy
```

In Windows:

```
C:\Users\PC> eb status
Environment details for: django-env
 Application name: django- deployment
 ...
 Status: Ready
 Health: Green
C:\Users\PC> eb deploy
```

Run eb status in your command prompt to make sure the environment initialization is complete. Then run eb deploy to upload your Django project to Amazon Web Service (AWS) Elastic Beanstalk server. This may take a few minutes.

Open the ES environment in the browser

Run the command eb open to see the web app in the browser deployed. You can also copy and paste the CNAM (ALLOWED_HOST) in the setting.py file in the browser to view the live site.

Accessing Django Admin in Deployment

We have to change the static files configuration to allow for Django style sheets. We can use the Django admin panel in deployment. Go to the setting.py and add STATIC_ROOT to the new directory serving the files. Comment on the STATICFILES_DIRS and then save the files.

Collect the Static in the CLI

Before that, you should reactivate your virtual environment. To activate your background, you should change your directory path to Script and then run activate. Activate this now run Python manage.py collectstatic and hit enter.
    In Window,

```
C:\Users\PC> python manage.py collectstatic
You need to have to collect static files at the
destination location as specified in your stings:
```

```
C:\Users\PC\static
This command overwrites the existing files.
Are you sure you like to do this?
Type 'yes' to continue, or 'no' to cancel: yes
435 static files copied to 'C:\Users\PC\static', 7
modified.
```

Run the collectstatic to your files from your static folder into the STATIC_ROOT folder. If you want to collect static files, type yes and wait for the files to be copied.

Again redeploy your project with eb deploy after deactivating your virtual environment. Once deployed, open the browser with your deployed project and go to the admin page now. It has the CSS in it.

Check the Django Web App from AWS

Login to your AWS and select the region where you deployed your project – then search for Elastic Beanstalk in the console. If you get it, click on it, and then your environments in that region should appear. There are various options in it that you can check: your website created date and time, the URL of your site, platform technologies like in this project we have used Python for building the website, last modification, and termination.

To terminate your website, select the Django-env, click the Actions to get dropdown menu, select terminate environment, enter the name of your domain to confirm "Django-deployment", and click terminate. Once you terminated it, you move to the Application name and select "Delete application". Enter the name of the Application and click delete. Your Application will be deleted entirely.

AZURE

It is a public cloud computing platform – with solutions including Infrastructure as a service (IaaS), Platform as a Service (PaaS), and Software as a Service (SaaS) that can be used for storage, analytics, networking, virtual computing, storage, networking, and so on. It can be used to replace your on-premise servers. With its massive set of features and functionalities and build for the Microsoft platform, Azure makes it easier for IT professionals to develop and manage enterprise, mobile, web, and Internet of Things (IoT) apps and applications.

Features of Cloud-Based Services

- **Availability of Virtual Machines**: With the Microsoft Azure IaaS facility, you benefit from virtualization and virtual machines. User can launch their general-purpose virtual machine developed in the Windows or Linux platform.

- **Availability of App Services**: This facility of Azure falls under the Azure PaaS Services section. You can quickly produce as well as manage your websites and business web applications. It is yet another of the greatest Microsoft Azure Features for web developers, mobile app developers, and online business owners.

Microsoft Azure Features Related to Mobile Services

Another one of the great features of Microsoft Azure Strength is the mobile services provided by the Platform. Have a look at each of them.

1. **Mobile Engagement Services**: You can easily monitor and manage the mobile user engagement that your Application is getting from the users. The Azure Mobile Services allows for real-time data analytics tracking that helps you take a deep dive. You also get a push notification to keep track of the significant user.

2. **Data Management**: The Azure search uses SDK APIs or REST to bring up text-search and a subset of OData's structured filters.

Azure enables handling data-intensive queries on datasets that exceed 1TB through its data warehousing service called SQL Data Warehouse.

- **Storage**: This category of Azure services provides us scalable cloud storage for structured and unstructured data and supports big data projects, persistent storage, and archival storage. Last but not least, we have a file service feature in the Microsoft Azure cloud. Through this feature of Microsoft Azure for business application data storage, you can store your data on the cloud by using the REST API and the SMB protocol.

Queue Services let programs communicate asynchronously by using queries.

- **Analytics**: These Azure services provide us with distributed analytics and storage, as well as features for real-time analytics, big data analytics, data lakes, Machine Learning (ML), business intelligence (BI), Internet of Things (IoT) data streams, and data warehousing.

- **Containers**: These Azure services will help an enterprise create, register, orchestrate, and manage vast volumes of containers in the Azure cloud, using common platforms such as Docker and Kubernetes.

- **Internet of Things**: These services will help users capture, monitor, and analyze IoT data from sensors and other devices. Services include notifications, analytics, monitoring, and support for coding and execution.

- **Databases**: This category includes Database as a Service (DBaaS) offering for SQL and NoSQL and other database instances – such as Azure Cosmos DB and Azure Database for PostgreSQL. It also includes Azure SQL Data Warehouse support, caching, and hybrid database integration and migration features.

DEPLOYING OUR DJANGO APP ONTO AZURE

First, ensure that your system has Python installed, and then create a virtual environment by running the command pip install virtualenv used pip3 instead of pip.

Now that we have it running nearby, let's deploy our first app onto Azure.

File Structure

Now, create the django_azure_demo folder. Afterward, run the cd django_azure_Demo to see the files out of the django_azure_Demo folder should have manage.py.

In the beginning, push your code to Github:

```
1. git init
2. git remote add origin https://github.com/YOUR
_USERNAME/YOUR_REPO_NAME
3.git pull origin master
4.git add -A
5. git commit -m "Initial commit."
6.git push origin master
```

- **Git inits**: Initialize your local repo as a git repo.

- **Git remote add origin**: link your local repo with the remote repo in Github.

- **Git pulls**: Pull the remote .gitignore Github created to your local repo.

- **Git add**: Add all files for staging (files are in processing mode).

- **Git commits**: Save changes to your repo by "committing" the as message "-m".

- **Git push**: Pushing them to Github; you can view your files in your Github account whatever the name is given to your repository.

Installing Azure

Create a free account at azure.com. The Django app will be deployed through Azure's web app services. To sort, we will create a resource from the upper left "Create a Resource" button. Click on the "Web App" button, but it isn't there; you can search for "Web App" in the search bar. If you are a student, then visit this link https://azure.microsoft.com/en-us/offers /ms-azr-0144p/.

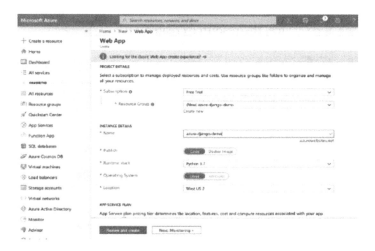

Azure deployment.

Fill out the information required. We will be calling our app azure-Django-demo. Make sure that when you are filling the configuration. Your system will be Linux, not windows.

Azure deployment.

Find the app service, the resource created.

Azure deployment.

The following should pop up on the screen:

Azure deployment.

Click on "Deployment Center" on the left sidebar (the light sidebar, not the dark). On-screen "Deployment Center" with three steps displayed pop-ups. You will first (1) deploy through GitHub, (2) use the App Service build service, and then (3) configure with your username, repo, and branch.

Azure deployment.

Finally, we will perform a few configuration changes to the Python app. In the search bar, you will find "Extensions".

Scroll to find and click the latest Python version (currently at Python 3.7). Once added, we will use the search bar to search for the "Configuration". Move to "General settings" in the Window that pops up on the screen, and change the Stack and Python Version to Python and 3.7, respectively.

Azure deployment.

You should be able to get your website at azure-django-demo.azure-ewebsites.net.

Azure Deployment Files

To deploy onto Azure, we will need one additional file, requrment.txt, which specifies the Azure package to install for your app to work. If you want to access the Azure app live, then add '*' in ALLOWED_HOST like ALLOWED_HOST = ['* '].

GIT

It is a free and open distributed version control system that lets you manage and hold onto the track of your source code history, and where Github is a cloud-based hosting service that collects Git repository. If you have an open-source that use Git, then Github is designed to help you better manage them. Why do we need both? You do not need Github to use Git, but you cannot use Github without using Git.

- **Installing Git**: You can download it from their formal site and install it on your PC. Git has its two-mode modes of use – a bash scripting shelly (command line) and a graphical user interface (GUI).

- **Configure Github Credentials**:: Configure your local Git installations to use your Github credentials by entering the following:

o git config –global user. Name "Enter your name".

o Git config –global user-email "email_address".

- **Clone a Github Repository**: Go to your repository on Github. In the top right above, open the Clone or download dropdown menu. Copy the URL for cloning over HTTPS.

- **Setting Up a Local Repository**: Open your project location and open the Git bash for the same path. It can be downloaded from the internet. Then run these lines of code one by one:

  o **git inits**: It will initialize Git as creating .git name folder in your project.

  o **git add**: For adding all the files, run this command and manually use "git add folder/filename".

  o **git commit –m**: 'First Commit done'.

  o git remote add origin "PASTE THE URL OF YOUR NEW REPOSITORY IN GITHUB" example, https://github .com/project_name. Git.

  o **git push –u origin**: It will add your files in the git repository of your account.

  o **git status**: Check your current level.

CHAPTER SUMMARY

In this chapter, we covered the deployment of Django using the various cloud platforms like AWS Elastic Beanstalk, Microsoft Azure, Github, and Git. We have multiple options for deployment over the internet, free as well as paid. Paid will have more features than free, so if you're a beginner, first go for free and then for paid after getting familiar with their environment.

Create Quiz Web App with Python Django

IN THIS CHAPTER

➢ Getting to know the basics of Django

➢ Todo application overview

➢ Project code

In this chapter, beginners will learn the baiscs of Python Django before starting any web-based application or development. It is important to have a good understanding of the basics before attempting any projects.

Before we discuss Django, let's first look at why we need a web framework. A web framework is a server application framework that is designed to support dynamic websites. With the help of this framework, you don't have to bother about web development. There are various web development frameworks available on the market. Some of them are as follows:

REACT, FLASK, RUBY ON RAILS, ETC.

One of the main points of Django is that it is built on Python. It follows the principle of DRY – "Don't Repeat Yourself". It takes care of user content administration, authentication, site maps, and many more. It is highly secure. It helps all the other developers avoid many common security mistakes, such as SQL injection, cross-site scripting, csrf/xsrf, and click-jacking.

DOI: 10.1201/9781003310495-11

221

It is pretty scalable, like using a shared nothing pattern, which means you can add hardware at any stage – database servers, caching servers, or applications servers. It has various other advantages: it has an automatic administration interface, ORM, RSS feeds, and many more.

It builds websites dynamically, it is extremely fast, and it is SEO optimized.

HOW TO CREATE A QUIZ LIST APP IN PYTHON DJANGO

Let's develop our own Quiz App Project in Django and let others test their knowledge using the quiz. This will help you understand the basics of the Django Python framework and how to design the frontend and backend parts.

Everyone likes to attempt a quiz, checking scores at the end, and seeing how much time it takes to attempt to make an answer. Have you ever tried to make a quiz that othe people can play using some of your programming knowledge?

If you are a beginner at Django, then it is the perfect project for you. It will improve your frontend skills, including HTML, CSS, and so on.

Purpose

The objective of our project is to make a quiz that has different topics using the Python Django framework. Good knowledge of Django and frontend skills is enough for the project.

Project Prerequisites

- **Text-Editor**: Any text-editors like Visual Code, Brackets, PyCharm, and so on. You can download these editors from the internet. These editors can help you to understand the structure most thoroughly.

- **Python3**: You should have the latest version of Python in your system; visit the Python Official Website to get that.

Note: You can easily follow this project to understand the basics of Python and learn about loops, functions, classes, etc., for advanced knowledge, you will learn about bash and command lines.

Virtual Environment

It acts as a dependency to Python-related projects. It is self-contained and found in all Python-related packages and the required version. It is highly recommended to create and execute a Django application in a separate environment. Python provides the tool virtualenv to create an isolated Python environment.

Install-Package
Create a Virtual Environment (run these commands in the terminal of the same folder where you want to create the Django project).

```
C:\Users\PC> python -m venv Virtual_name
```

Change the directory

```
C:\Users\PC> cd Virtual_name
```

Activate the environment: Virtual_name/Scripts/activate.

```
C:\Users\PC> cd Virtual_name
C:\Users\PC\Virtual_name> cd Scripts.
C:\Users\PC\Virtual_name\Scripts> activate.
 (env) C:\Users\PC\Virtual_name\Scripts>
```

In the same folder, install Django using pip install Django.

```
(Virtual_name) C:\Users\PC\Virtual_name\Scripts>
pip install django
```

The installation steps at one place; have a look at it for better understanding.

```
C:\Users\PC\dd>python -m venv Virtual_env
C:\Users\PC\dd>cd Virtual_env
C:\Users\PC\Quiz\Virtual_env>cd Scripts
C:\Users\PC\Quiz\Virtual_env\Scripts>activate
(Virtual_env) C:\Users\PC\Quiz\Virtual_env\
Scripts>pip install django
Collecting django
 Using cached Django-3.2.9-py3-none-any.whl (7.9 MB)
Collecting asgiref<4,>=3.3.2
 Using cached asgiref-3.4.1-py3-none-any.whl (25 kB)
Collecting sqlparse>=0.2.2
 Using cached sqlparse-0.4.2-py3-none-any.whl (42 kB)
```

```
Collecting pytz
 Using cached pytz-2021.3-py2.py3-none-any.whl
(503 kB)
Installing collected packages: sqlparse, pytz,
asgiref, Django
Successfully installed asgiref-3.4.1 Django-3.2.9
pytz-2021.3 sqlparse-0.4.2
WARNING: You are using pip version, .i.e, 21.2;
however, version 21.3.1 is available now.
You should going to upgrading via the 'c:\users\
dell\dd\virtual_env\scripts\python.exe -m pip
install --upgrade pip' command.
```

1. Creating a Django project:

The first step in creating your project is done by using:

```
(Virtual_env) C:\Users\PC\Quiz\Virtual_env\
Scripts>cd ..
  (Virtual_env) C:\Users\PC\Quiz\Virtual_env>cd ..
  (Virtual_env) C:\Users\PC\Quiz\>django-admin
startproject Quiz
```

Change your directory using the cd command:

```
(Virtual_env) C:\Users\PC\Quiz\>cd Quiz
```

You have finished the installation process; now, create the app using the command in the command prompt:

```
(Virtual_env) C:\Users\PC\Quiz\Quiz>django-admin
startapp quizapp
```

The whole code at one place:

```
   Virtual_env) C:\Users\PC\Quiz\Virtual_env\
Scripts>cd ..
  (Virtual_env) C:\Users\PC\Quiz\Virtual_env>cd ..
   (Virtual_env) C:\Users\PC\Quiz\>django-admin
startproject Quiz
   (Virtual_env) C:\Users\PC\Quiz\>cd Quiz
```

```
(Virtual_env) C:\Users\PC\Quiz\Quiz>django-admin
startapp quizapp
     (Virtual_env) C:\Users\\PC\Quiz\Quiz>
```

2. The second step is to let our project know about our newly created app by changing the Quiz/settibg.py INSTALLED_APP section.

```
INSTALLED_APPS = [
  'django.contrib.admin',
  'django.contrib.auth',
  'django.contrib.contenttypes',
  'django.contrib.sessions',
  'django.contrib.messages',
  'django.contrib.staticfiles',
  'quizapp'
]
```

Changing in Our Models
Django uses the default database "SQLite", which is lightweight and on projects for small projects, which is fine for this project. Its uses OBJECT RELATIONAL MAPPER (ORM), making it easy to work with the database.

```
from Django.DB import models
# Create your models here.
class QuestionsModel(models.Model):
  question = models.CharField(max_length=200,nul
l=True)
  option_one = models.CharField(max_length=200,nul
l=True)
  option_two = models.CharField(max_length=200,nul
l=True)
  option_three = models.CharField(max_length=200,nul
l=True)
  option_four = models.CharField(max_length=200,nul
l=True)
  answer = models.CharField(max_length=200,null=True)
    def __str__(self):
    return self.question
```

In the above code, we import the model from Django.db. It is a built-in module of Django with various packages like models to use in our project. The database tables are created with the help of class keywords in "modye.py".

Inside the model.py, you need to create a new model named "Questionmodel". This is a class that becomes a database table that currently inherits the model. Models. Every field must have a Field type like the above. We have CharField(). It is a text-based column and accepts "max_length" of 200. Like CharField, we can use TextField, which contains detailed text, and IntegerField, which contains a number. As shown above, we have questions with four options with correct answers. Each has a type field. The double underscore (str) method is defined, which overrides the model's default in the admin panel and returns the name of the actual "title" instead of some object.

Making a Migration

python manage.py makes migration a first step process, and reads as "model.py". It introduces a brand new folder called "migrations" where there are files name "0001_initial.py" which are portable across the database.

```
C:\Users\Dell\Desktop\Quiz\Myquiz> python manage.py
makemigrations
Did you rename questionsmodel.option_one to
questionsmodel.option_o (a CharField)? [y/N] y
Migrations for 'quizapp':
 quizapp\migrations\0002_auto_20211106_1649.py
  - Rename field option_one on questionsmodel to
option_o
```

Migrating to the Database

This is the second step where "python manage.py migrate" reads the newly created folder "migrations" and creates the database, and it involves the database when there is a change in the model.

```
C:\Users\PC\Desktop\Quiz\Myquiz> python manage.py
migrate
Operations to perform:
 Apply all migrations: admin, auth, contenttypes,
quiz app, sessions
```

```
Running migrations:
 Applying quizapp.0002_auto_20211106_1649... OK
```

Registering to the Admin

Let's move to "admin.py" and import the models called "QuestionsModel" by using "from .models import QuestionsModel".

```
from django.contrib import admin
from .models import *
# Register your models here.
admin.site.register(QuestionsModel)
```

Creating Superuser and Viewing in the Admin Panel

You need to create a superuser before accessing the "admin" panel. To do so, use python manage.py to create a superuser.

```
C:\Users\PC\Desktop\Quiz\Myquiz> python manage.py
createsuperuser
Username (leave blank to use 'dell'): Quiz
Error: That username is already taken.
Username (leave blank to use 'dell'): quiz
Email address:
Password:
Password (again):
The password is similar to the username.
This password is short. It must contain at least
eight characters.
Bypass password validation and create a user anyway?
[y/N]: y
Superuser created successfully.
```

Now run your server in the terminal by using the command python manage.py run server.

```
C:\Users\PC\Desktop\Quiz\Myquiz> python manage.py
run server
Watching for file changes with StatReloader
Performing system checks...
System check identified no issues (0 silenced).
November 06, 2021 - 17:06:37
```

```
Django version 3.1.4, using settings 'Myquiz.
settings'.
Run development server at http://127.0.0.1:8000/
Quit the server with CTRL-BREAK.
```

We set up the basic configuration of our application. Now we will move to the application setup. This is the basic structure of files in the Django project.

```
>Quiz (folder name)
  >Myquiz (folder name)
    > __pycache__
    __init__.py
    asgi.py
    setting.py
    urls.py
    wsgi.py
  >MyQuiz (project name)
    >quizapp (application name)
      >__pychache__
      >migratons (migrations files)
      >templates
        >home.html
        >login.html
        >register.html
        >navbar.html
  db.sqlite3
  manage.py
```

Making and Changing the Templates
Let's make a templates folder that generally holds "HTML" and contains their templating language called "jinja2". The folder needs to name "templates", which is the convention.

```
>templates
  >home.html
  >login.html
  >register.html
  >navbar.html
```

You can see there is syntax related to "HTML Hyper Text Mark-up Language". You have created various HTML files for our Quiz App.

1. Base.html

2. Home.html

3. Login.html

4. Navbar.html

5. Register.html

6. Result.html

First, discuss the code of Base.html – where you can add all the static files links like CSS, JavaScript, etc. and attach those files inside the <head> tag in <link> tag.

BASE.HTML

```
{# HTML5 Declaration #}
{% load static %}
<html>
  <head>
    <title>
      Quiz with Django
    </title>
    <link rel="stylesheet" href="https://maxcdn
.bootstrapcdn.com/bootstrap/4.0.0/css/bootstrap.min
.css" integrity="sha384-Gn5384xqQ1aoWXA+058RXPxPg6f
y4IWvTNh0E263XmFcJlSAwiGgFAW/dAiS6JXm"
crossorigin="anonymous">
  </head>
  <body>
    {% include 'navbar.html' %}
    {% block content %}
    {% endblock %}
    <br>
      <script src="https://code.jquery.com/jquery-
3.2.1.slim.min.js" integrity="sha384-KJ3o2DKtIkvY
IK3UENzmM7KCkRr/rE9/Qpg6aAZGJwFDMVNA/GpGFF93hXpG5
KkN" crossorigin="anonymous"></script>
    <script src="https://cdn.jsdelivr.net/npm/popper
.js@1.16.0/dist/umd/popper.min.js" integrity="sha3
84-Q6E9RHvbIyZFJoft+2mJbHaEWldlvI9IOYy5n3zV9zzTtmI
```

```
3UksdQRVvoxMfooAo" crossorigin="anonymous"></
script>
  <script src="https://maxcdn.bootstrapcdn.com/
bootstrap/4.0.0/js/bootstrap.min.js" integrity="sha3
84-JZR6Spejh4U02d8jOt6vLEHfe/JQGiRRSQQxSfFWpi1MquV
dAyjUar5+76PVCmYl" crossorigin="anonymous"></
script>
  </body>
</html>
```

In base.html, the first step while creating templates for the project is to create the base template. It is used to set the top navigation bar and the footer, and provide the body canvas for any page. By using this base template, we can give a traditional look to our HTML page with any duplicate code. The base.html files can have huge lines of code.

The top topline shows that we are commenting our text like that {# add any text}. The {% load static %} tag is used to add load in the static folder in the base file. This is the key part of the templating language. It provides you with the specific parts of the file that can be changed by pages that extend it. Any page that extends the base.html could easily change the title by writing {%block title %} Add Text {% end block title %}.

- {% include 'navbar.html' %}

Include will help you to extend the page it always writes on top of the code.

- {% block content %}

In between the block, you can add your HTML code for rendering.

- {% end block %}

This helps a lot more to extend your template and reduce the repetition of the common code like style sheets, JavaScript code, and so on.

LOGIN.HTML

```
{% extends 'dependencies.html' %}
{% load static%}
{% block content %}
```

```
<div class="container jumbotron">
  <form method="POST" action="">
    {% csrf_token %}
    <p><input type="text" name="username"
placeholder="Username..."></p>
    <p><input type="password" name="password"
placeholder="Password..." ></p>
    <input class="btn btn-primary" type="submit"
value="login">
    <p>Do not have an account<a href='{% url
'register' %}'>Register</a></p>
  </form>
</div>
{% endblock %}
```

The login page will describe the login form for users so that they can enter their login details to get access to their accounts. {% extends 'dependenices.html' %} extends the code by adding the dependenices.html on top. Dependenice.html is the file where we get all the common code included in every template page. {%load static %} will help to load the static folder; static folder includes the files like CSS, images, or others. In <div> tags, I have used the class attributes with container jumbotron in them. We get it from the Bootstrap CDN link in our dependenices.html file. CDN (content delivery network) has all the classes defined in Bootstrap. By adding this link, you get access to it. Bootstrap helps you to make the web page more attractive. Next, we have < Form> tags with method POST. It is secure to store data over the internet. {% csrf_token %} helps to prevent us from the various attack from SQL injection so that nobody can get access to your site. The Form has two input tags which take username and password. It also has some attributes like name defining, the name of the field like if you want to store the data, you can refer the name to use, placeholder defines the name which shows inside the input tags on the browser. The button is used to click the event. When you press any button, something will happen. Below the button, we have an anchor tag that mainly works as routing. It will redirect us to the registration page; at last, we have the end of the block. The whole code should be in the block section; otherwise, your code will not render.

LOGIN PAGE

Figure 11.1 shows the login page.

FIGURE 11.1   Login page.

- **templates > Register.html**

```
{% extends 'dependencies.html' %}
{% load static %}
{% block content %}
<div class="container jumbotron">
  <form method="POST" action="" >
    {% csrf_token %}
    {{form.as_p}}
      <input class="btn btn-primary" type="submit"
value="register here">
  </form>
</div>
{% end block %}
```

The register page will describe the register form for users so that they can enter their login details to get access to their accounts. {% extends 'dependenices.html' %} extends the code by adding the dependenices .html on top. Dependenice.html is the file where we get all the common codes included in every template page. {%load static %} will help to load the static folder; static folder includes the files like CSS, images, or others. In <div> tags, I have used the class attributes with the container, jumbotron, similar to the login page. The register form is slightly different from the login page here. We have used the {{Form.as_p }} that means we have to use the advance forms template like it will return the fields of the Form In paragraph like each data is wrapped up with the paragraph <p> tag. {% csrf_token %} token is required for the data storage or retrieving.

REGISTER PAGE

Figure 11.2 shows the register page.

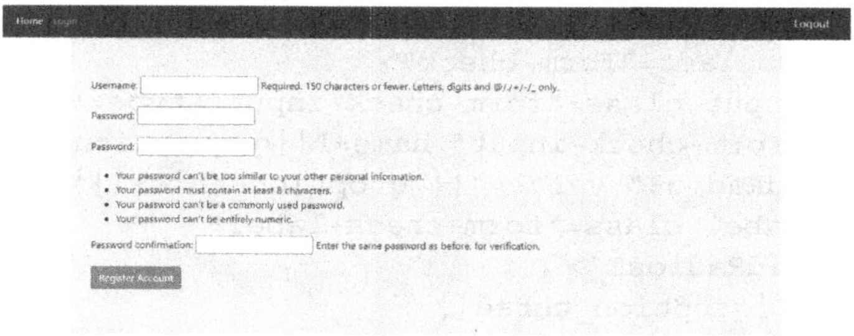

FIGURE 11.2   Registration page.

- **templates > home.html**

```
{% extends 'dependencies.html' %}
{% block content %}
{% load static %}
<div class="container ">
<h1>Quiz</h1>
 <form method='post' action=''>
  {% csrf_token %}
  {% for q in questions%}
  <div class="form-group">
   <label for="question">{{q.question}}</label>
  </div>
  <div class="form-check">
    <div class="form-check">
      <input type="radio" class="form-check-input" na
me="{{q.question}}" id="gridRadio1" value="{{
q.option_one }}" checked>
      <label class="form-check-label"
for="gridRadios1">
        {{q.option_one}}
      </label>
    </div>
    <div class="form-check">
      <input type="radio" class="form-check-input"
name="{{q.question}}" id="gridRadio2" value="{{
q.option_two }}">
      <label class="form-check-label"
for="gridRadios2">
        {{q.option_two}}
      </label>
```

```
    </div>
    <div class="form-check">
       <input class="form-check-input" type="radio"
class="form-check-input" name="{{q.question}}"
id="gridRadio3" value="{{ q.option_three }}">
       <label class="form-check-label"
for="gridRadios1">
          {{q.option_three}}
       </label>
    </div>
    <div class="form-check">
       <input type="radio" class="form-check-input"
name="{{q.question}}" id="gridRadio4" value="{{
q.option_four }}">
       <label class="form-check-label"
for="gridRadios2">
          {{q.option_four}}
       </label>
    </div>
    <br>
  </div>
  {% endfor %}
  <br>
  <button type="submit" class="btn btn-
primary">Submit</button>
 </form>
  {% block script %}
    <script>
    console.log('hello world')
       </script>
  {% endblock script %}
</div>
{% endblock %}
```

The homepage contains the code of the root URL of the application that means when somebody hits the URL, the very first page will be the root URL which is the home page. In url.py, this will look like a path ('', home,name='home'). The first empty parameter means that you are referring to the root URL. {%load static %} will help to load the static folder; static folder includes the files like CSS, images, or others. In <div> tags, I have used the class attributes with jumbotron. To start with the method, POST adds {%csrf_token%} after the form tag and then applies over the form inputs like {% for q in questions %} we have used Jinja templates expressions. <div> tag has class form-group and bootstrap class <label > is used to add label for the text. {{q.question}} is a Jinja template from where we can get our value on the browser. The Jinja template expression will not show on the screen. Only the text using this { { } } bracket will show. Basically, q.question as q is the data provides for loop and question the field which is model's fields. This is the way you can get the value from the database. All the values are fetching in this way only. Now end the blocks that you have opened.

HOME PAGE

Figure 11.3 shows the home page.

- **templates > navbar.html**

```
{% load static %}
<style>
 .greet{
  font-size: 18px;
  color: #fff;
  margin-right: 20px;
 }
</style>
<nav class="navbar navbar-expand-lg navbar-dark
bg-dark">
 <button type="button" class="navbar-toggler" da
ta-toggle="collapse" data-target="#navbarbnav" aria-
controls="navbarNav" aria-expanded="false" aria-
label="Toggle navigation">
```

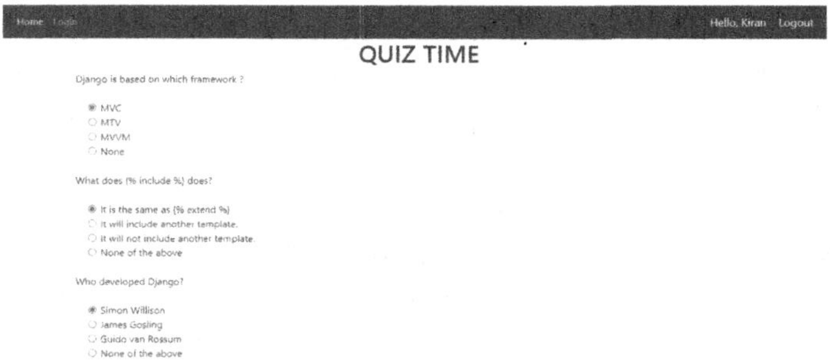

FIGURE 11.3   Home page.

```
    <span class="navbar-toggler-icon"></span>
   </button>
   <div class="collapse navbar-collapse"
id="navbarnav">
    <ul class="navbar-nav">
      <li class="nav-item active">
     <a class="nav-link" href="{% url 'home' %}">
Home </a>
   </li>
   </li>
   <li class="nav-item active">
      </li>
   <li class="nav-item">
     <a class="nav-link" href="{% url 'login' %}">
Login </a>
   </li>
   </ul>
   </div>
   {% if user.is_authenticated %}
   <span class="greet"> Hello, {{request.user}} </
span>
   {% endif %}
   <span><a class="greet" href="{% url 'logout' %}">
Logout </a></span>
   </nav
```

Navbar is the common bar added on the top of every single page. You can add this file by {% include 'navbar.html' %}. It will automatically add to the top of every page. It should be one top. In this file, we have added Bootstrap Navbar so that our text looks good and we can easily manage, add our content. Open navbar tag adds the class attributes in it. This navbar is responsive, meaning when the screen gets smaller, all the content will be hidden and will show behind the button. Then whenever you hit that button, all the navbar options will work and show as dropdown menus. Next, you have a button inside the navbar class. Its type is the button, data-toggle is collapsed, and the target id is mentioned so that when the screen is small, the button overlap the navbar, while hitting the button, the target refers to the id that would be same in all cases, otherwise nothing will happen. To run this whole code, you should add Bootstrap CSS, javaScript files named as

1. "href="https://stackpath.bootstrapcdn.com/bootstrap/4.5.1/css/bootstrap.min.css".

2. "https://cdn.jsdelivr.net/npm/popper.js@1.16.1/dist/umd/popper.min.js"

3. "src="https://stackpath.bootstrapcdn.com/bootstrap/4.5.1/js/bootstrap.min.js"

Code only runs when it is properly added to your file. Then we have div class with the id NavbarNav for toggling on the small screen. Next, in the <li> tag, we keep the nav-item and active class to tell the browser that this is the nav-item link, add the <a> tags with class nav-link; href tells the template that this is the link for navigation. Similarly, other navigation links in Jinja are written as {% URL 'home' %}: the first argument is URL pattern name and the next argument is used as an argument in the URL.

The next line lets you know whether the user is authenticated or not. The code {% if user.is_authenticated %} describes that if the user is authenticated, it will check authentication using the built-in method, i.e., it is_authenticated if the user is authenticated, and then the next lines of code will run. It will show the authenticate user name {{request. User}}. Always remember to end the if block; the logout option is next to it, which will redirect the user to the root.

- **templates > result.html**

```
{% extends 'dependencies.html' %}
{% block content %}
<div class="container ">
    <div class="card-column">
    <div class="card" align="centre ">
    <div class="card-body">
      <h5 class="card-title">Score: {{ score
}}</h5>
        <p class="card-text">Percentage: {{ percent
}}</p>
        <p class="card-text">Correct answers: {{
correct }}</p>
        <p class="card-text">Incorrect answers: {{
wrong }}</p>
```

```
        <p class="card-text">Total questions: {{
total }}</p>
        <h5>All the best for next quiz!</h5>
      </div>
    </div>
  </div>
</div>
{% end block %}
```

The above code will show you the result in sequence. The result is processed in the view.py in-home function. Whenever there is no False condition that occurs, the user will redirect after the successful execution of the code {{ variable }}. Variables like score, percent, correct, wrong, and the total will be shown using the syntax.

RESULT PAGE

Figure 11.4 shows the result page.

url.py

```
from Django. contrib import admin
from Django.URLs import path
from Django.URLs.conf import include
from quiz app.URLs import *
urlpatterns = [
  path('admin/', admin.site.urls),
  path('',include('quizapp.urls')),
]
```

1. From Django. contrib import admin

   It is automatically looking for an admin module in each application and importing them when it gets imported.

FIGURE 11.4   Show your quiz result.

2. From Django.URLs import path

The path function contains the Django.URL module. It is used for routing URLs to the appropriate view function within an application using dispatcher (expression).

3. From Django.URLs.conf import include

A function that takes full import path to another URLconf module where include can be added. The dot (.) operator, in this case, is shortcuts accessing the current package.

4. From quiz app.URLs import *

quiz app.URLs are the URL file of the quiz app application, so here we are just importing them to make them in use.

url.py

```
from django.urls import path
from quizapp.views import *
from django.conf import settings
from django.conf.urls.static import static
urlpatterns = [
  path('', home ,name='home'),
  path(' login/ ', loginpage ,name='login'),
  path(' logout/ ', logoutpage ,name='logout'),
  path(' register/ ', registerpage ,name='register'),
]

if settings.DEBUG:
  urlpatterns += static(settings.MEDIA_URL,
  document_root=settings.MEDIA_ROOT)
```

In url.py, we have an essential module that needs to be imported:

1. From Django.URLs import path

The path function contains the Django.URL module. It is used for routing URLs to the appropriate view function within an application using dispatcher (expression).

2. From quiz app. views import *

quiz app.URLs are the URL file of the quiz app application, so here we are just importing them to make them in use.

3. From Django.conf import settings

It abstracts the default and site-specific setting also presents a single interface. The setting file holds the value that your web app needs to work your database setting, static files, API key, Secret key, and a bunch of stuff.

4. From django.conf.urls.static import static

For setting, static needs to introduce the Django.contrib.static in url.py file to make a path like STATIC_ROOT, MEDIA_ROOT, and MEDIA_URL and STATIC_URL are for URL.

Urlpattern is the tuple where you define the mapping between the URLs and View. You are merging the path of MEDIA here for adding images in the project.

form.py

```
from django.forms import ModelForm
from .models import *
from django.contrib.auth.forms import
UserCreationForm
from django.contrib.auth.models import User
class createuserform(UserCreationForm):
    class Meta:
      model=User
      fields=['username','password']
```

In form.py, we will learn how to make the Form using built-in Form, i.e., UserCreationForm. First, import the package, and then from the package, import the particular module for use in your project. So from Django, Forms is the package, and the module name is ModelForm that we use in form.py. Second, we import all the models of the particular application, (*) is the symbol that fetches all the models from that file. There is no need to get them manually from the .model import create user form.

Next, we have UserCreationForm and User. These are built-in modules in Django. Both have various data fields like username, password, email, confirm password, and so on. Remember, you have to write the model in class, not in function. Inside the create user form, we have the class Meta, which provides us with all information related to Meta (brief information about data). It has various fields like the model, fields, and so on, but here we have only two models that define the model of that Form, like where the Form data get stored and what kinds of attributes the Form has. Next, we have fields username and password. Our Form has only two fields: the username and password. With it, the user is able to log in with their own credentials. There UserCreationForm overrides the fields of the other Form in it. If you would like to use all the fields, then prefer a piece of code, fields="__all__". These are used to take all the input at once with Form.

view.py

```
from django.shortcuts import redirect,render
from django.contrib.auth import
login,logout,authenticate
from .forms import *
from .models import *
from django.http import HttpResponse
from django.contrib.auth.models import auth
# Create your views here.
def home(request):
  if request.method == 'POST':
    print(request.POST)
    questions=QuestionsModel.objects.all()
    score=0
    wrong=0
    correct=0
    total=0
    for q in questions:
      total+=1
      print(request.POST.get(q.question))
      print(q.answer)
      print()
      if q.answer == request.POST.get(q.question):
        score+=10
        correct+=1
      else:
        wrong+=1
    percent = score/(total*10) *100
    context = {
      'score':score,
      'correct':correct,
      'wrong':wrong,
      'percent':percent,
```

```
      'total':total
    }
    return render(request,'result.html',context)
  else:
    questions=QuestionsModel.objects.all()
    context = {
      'questions':questions
    }
    return render(request,'home.html',context)
def registerPage(request):
  if request.user.is_authenticated:
    return redirect('home')
  else:
    form = createuserform()
    if request.method=='POST':
      form = createuserform(request.POST)
      if form.is_valid() :
        user=form.save()
        return redirect('login')
    context={
      'form':form,
    }
    return render(request,'register.html',context)
def loginPage(request):
  if request.user.is_authenticated:
    return redirect('home')
  else:
    if request.method=="POST":
    username=request.POST.get('username')
    password=request.POST.get('password')
    user=authenticate(request,username=username,p
assword=password)
    if user is not None:
      login(request,user)
      return redirect('/')
    context={}
    return render(request,'login.html',context)
def logoutPage(request):
  auth.logout(request)
  return redirect('/')
```

Here in the view.py, you will get the same import of module as above; before getting into the code, let's discuss the import section of the view. py file:

1. **From Django. shortcuts import redirect, render:** This piece of code contains the important functionality in the project while rendering the text to the template and redirecting to the exact URL for making the site dynamic. You can get all the redirect and return from Django. Shortcuts.

2. **From django. contrib.auth import logout, authenticate, login:** This will help you to make your view safe. Once the user is registered, then only the same user can access the site. Login, logout helps to pass the authenticated user with authentication. In the last chapters, you have learned about the admin panel where all the data are stored.

3. **From .forms import *:** Form play a vital role here because you can get your form data directly by importing it in the view.py file. Form data can only be stored when the user enters the details and hits the POST method. That is why in every Form, we always write if method == POST; this code will only run when the method match.

4. **From .models import *:** The model file import like this when a user enters its data in the Form, the foms.py runs, and data will be saved when the save() method execute, the below code is the example of save method.

   - if request.method=='POST':
   - form = createuserform(request.POST)
   - if form.is_valid() :
   - user=form.save()
   - return redirect('login')

   When the user hits the button, the request method matches the user value, which we will get from the createuserform(request. POST) saved in the form variable; in the next line, check whether the code is valid: if Form.is_valid() return True, then user details stores in the database link with the database after the successful running of code windows which redirect to the login page.

5. **From Django.HTTP import HttpResponse:** HttpResponce returns the text to the client back to the browser. Whenever a request comes into play, it is handled by the Middleware and rendered by the HttpResponse.

6. **From django.contrib.auth.Models import auth:** contrib. Auth in your INSTALLED_APP setting.py file will ensure the four default common permissions – add, delete, change, and view.

This is the common importing model in the view.py.

All the logic of the Django project should be written in separate functions. We have different functions for each page so that everything looks better and runs in the proper way. Have a look over the code for the home page.

So, the home function has been requested. The method will first run only when you hit the POST method. After that, you get all the data stored in the Database with QuestionsModel.object.all() where all methods help you to get the stored data and render to the browser score, and the wrong, correct, total are variables to store some values, and then the loop will run over the question and store in q variable total which will increase by 1 for each question if the question's answer is correct and the score will increase by 10 and correct value will increase by 1, and if the answer is wrong, the wrong variable will increase by 1. When the quiz is over, the player gets a score with their percentage. The context variable gets the value as key-value pairs (dictionaries), the way to write the dictionaries like this {'key': 'value'}. After the completion of code successfully, the render() will return the result.html with the context. If anything goes wrong, for example a syntax error or other error occurs, it will simply return the question and render it to the home page.

So, the register page() method has been requested as a parameter. Next, this will let you know that if the user is authenticated, there is no need to login as it simply redirects you to the home.html; however, if the user is new to the site, then they first have to register, and they get the Form.

Login page() has the same parameter as register because the request is generated by the user. When the user is already authenticated, this will be checked by the authenticate method to see if the user name and password exist or not. When the user does not exist, this will redirect to the root, which is home.html.

On the logout page(), the method name auth. Logout (request) is used for logging out only if the user is logged in. This option will only come when the user is authenticated.

app.py

```
From Django. apps import AppConfig
class QuizappConfig(AppConfig):
  default_auto_field = 'django.db.models.BigAutoF
ield'
  name = 'quizapp'
```

It is a configuration that is common to all Django applications. The AppConfig used to configure the application has a path attribute. The name of the class is in-app. Y is similar to the name of your application. Its word letter must be capital pass parentheses add AppConfig . the default_ Auto_field is an attribute and the default value is DEFAULT_AUTO_ FIELD if BigAutoField. BigAutoField is an auto-incrementing primary key according to the available IDs like AutoField.

WHAT IS THE PURPOSE OF THIS PROJECT?

In this project you have learned Python and Django from scratch. It has shown you how to make syntax and logic. Now you are able to make your own project. The concepts we have used in this project are related to authentication, model, templating, forms, and view with static files.

So this is our Quiz App, here we will tell you the reason why we prefer to make these kinds of projects in any language. When going for a job, one should have at least one project in their hand so that they can get a better chance of getting a job in the company. Without practice you cannot code properly. So our point of view regarding this is that you can learn and practice the basic of the language, understand the syntax more clearly, and you can also add new things to it. Once you get the entire point, try to make the project but with some variation. Have a good command over the basics, learn some advanced functionalities like class, method, inheritance, and so on. Instead of using the function, use class in a better way because the class is callable in nature. In the future, your small project will help you a lot more.

Project To-Do List

IN THIS CHAPTER

> ➢ Getting to know about Django

> ➢ Quiz application overview

> ➢ Project code

In this chapter, we will be creating a To-Do app that is fully scalable and runs on a platform independent basis. This will give you a head start for Django with the proper understanding of basic things.

Before understanding Django, let's first know why we need a web framework? A web framework is a server application framework that is designed to support dynamic websites. With the help of these frameworks, you don't have to bother about web development. There are various web development frameworks available on the market. Some of them are as follows:

REACT, FLASK, RUBY ON RAILS, ETC.

One of the main points of Django is that it is built on Python. It follows the principle of DRY – "Don't Repeat Yourself." It takes care of user content administration, authentication, site maps, and many more. It is highly secure. It helps all beginners and developers avoid many common

DOI: 10.1201/9781003310495-12

security mistakes, such as SQL injection, cross-site scripting, csrf/xsrf, and click-jacking.

It is pretty scalable, like using a shared-nothing architecture, which means you can add hardware at any level – database servers, caching servers, or applications servers. It has various other advantages: it has an intuitive administration interface, ORM, RSS feeds, and many more.

It builds websites dynamically, it is extremely fast, and SEO optimized.

HOW TO CREATE A TO-DO LIST APP IN PYTHON DJANGO

A list that keeps track of all the tasks you perform in a single day is called a to-do list. It is a manageable way to complete tasks on time. It makes the users responsible for also knowing the value of time. Today we will be creating a to-do list application using the Django framework. The main motive of this to-do list is to get some knowledge of Python syntax and Django CRUD. It has some basic functionality like Create, Read, Update, and Delete. Users can add their tasks and also delete them.

If you know the fundamentals of Django and Python well, then you are good to go with this project. Here are the steps to start this project.

1. **Install Python:** Before we go forward, ensure you have Python installed in your system. If you do not have Python, install Python from its official site.

2. Add environment variable in the environment variable set so that you won't get any problem regarding the path.

3. Create a folder and then create a virtual environment in it using Python –m venv Virtual_env.

4. Activate the virtual environment when it has been installed in your folder.

5. Move to directory Scripts, using the cd command.

6. The run activates in the folder.

7. It will let you move to the end of the project, where you have to install your Django using pip install Django.

8. After installation of Django, move back to the project folder using cd .. twice.

9. In the root folder, you have to create the Project Directory using admin-Django start project TodoApp.

10. Use the admin-Django startapp Todo.

Here's the whole code in one place:

```
C:\Users\PC\dd>python -m venv Virtual_env
C:\Users\PC\dd>cd Virtual_env
C:\Users\PC\Quiz\Virtual_env>cd Scripts
C:\Users\PC\Quiz\Virtual_env\Scripts>activate
(Virtual_env) C:\Users\PC\Quiz\Virtual_env\
Scripts>pip install django
Collecting django
 Using cached Django-3.2.9-py3-none-any.whl (7.9 MB)
Collecting asgiref<4,>=3.3.2
 Using cached asgiref-3.4.1-py3-none-any.whl (25 kB)
Collecting sqlparse>=0.2.2
 Using cached sqlparse-0.4.2-py3-none-any.whl (42 kB)
Collecting pytz
 Using cached pytz-2021.3-py2.py3-none-any.whl (503 kB)
Installing collected packages: sqlparse, pytz,
asgiref, Django
Successfully installed asgiref-3.4.1 Django-3.2.9
pytz-2021.3 sqlparse-0.4.2
WARNING: You are using pip version 21.1.3; however,
version 21.3.1 is available.
You should consider upgrading via the 'c:\users\
dell\dd\virtual_env\scripts\python.exe -m pip
install --upgrade pip' command.
  Virtual_env) C:\Users\PC\Quiz\Virtual_env\
Scripts>cd ..
  (Virtual_env) C:\Users\PC\Quiz\Virtual_env>cd ..
    (Virtual_env) C:\Users\PC\Quiz\>django-admin
startproject Quiz
    (Virtual_env) C:\Users\PC\Quiz\>cd Quiz
    (Virtual_env) C:\Users\PC\Quiz\Quiz>django-admin
startapp quizapp
    (Virtual_env) C:\Users\\PC\Quiz\Quiz>
```

Creating Superuser and Viewing in the Admin Panel

You have to create a superuser before accessing the "admin" panel. To do so, use python manage.py create superuser.

```
C:\Users\PC\Desktop\Quiz\Myquiz> python manage.py
createsuperuser
Username (leave blank to use 'dell'): Quiz
Error: That username is already taken.
Username (leave blank to use 'dell'): quiz
Email address:
Password:
Password (again):
The password is too similar to the username.
This password is too short. It must contain at least
eight characters.
Bypass password validation and create a user anyway?
[y/N]: y
Superuser created successfully.
```

Making a Migration

python manage.py makemigrations is the first step of the process. It reads the "model.py" and creates a new folder called "migrations" where there is a file named "0001_initial.py" which is portable across the database.

```
C:\Users\Dell\Desktop\Quiz\Myquiz> python manage.py
makemigrations
Did you rename questionsmodel.option_one to
questionsmodel.option_o (a CharField)? [y/N] y
Migrations for 'quizapp':
 quizapp\migrations\0002_auto_20211106_1649.py
  - Rename field option_one on questionsmodel to
option_o
```

Migrating to the Database

This is the second step where "python manage.py migrate" reads the newly created folder "migrations" and creates the database, and it evolves the database when there is a change in the model.

```
C:\Users\PC\Desktop\Quiz\Myquiz> python manage.py
migrate
Operations to perform:
```

```
Apply all migrations: admin, auth, contenttypes,
quiz app, sessions
Running migrations:
 Applying quizapp.0002_auto_20211106_1649... OK
```

Migrate your files once you create your app. It will apply the migration to all the pending ones.

Now run your server in the terminal by using the command python manage.py runserver.

```
C:\Users\PC\Desktop\Quiz\Myquiz> python manage.py
runserver
Watching for file changes with StatReloader
Performing system checks...
System check identified no issues (0 silenced).
November 06, 2021 - 17:06:37
Django version 3.1.4, using settings 'Myquiz.
settings'.
Starting development server at
http://127.0.0.1:8000/
Quit the server with CTRL-BREAK.
```

After running all the command, your Django environment is set up. The Folder Structure:

```
>TodoListApp (folder name)
  >TodoListApp (folder name)
    > __pycache__
    __init__.py
    asgi.py
    setting.py
    urls.py
    wsgi.py
  >Todo (project name)
    >quizapp (application name)
      >__pychache__
      >migratons (migrations files)
      >templates
        >home.html
        >login.html
        >register.html
        >navbar.html
```

```
>base.html
>update.html
db.sqlite3
manage.py
```

The Template Directory is a directory in which all the HTML templates will render to show the output. Let's discuss each of the templates.

- **templates > Base.html**

```
{% load static %}
<!DOCTYPE html>
<html lang="en">
<head>
  <meta charset="UTF-8">
  <meta http-equiv="X-UA-Compatible"
content="IE=edge">
  <meta name="viewport" content="width=device-width,
initial-scale=1.0">
  <title> Django CRUD </title>
  <link rel="stylesheet" href="{% static 'myFile.c
ss' %}" />
  <link rel="stylesheet" href="https://maxcdn
.bootstrapcdn.com/bootstrap/4.0.0/css/bootstrap.min
.css" integrity="sha384-Gn5384xqQ1aoWXA+058RXPxPg6f
y4IWvTNh0E263XmFcJlSAwiGgFAW/dAiS6JXm"
crossorigin="anonymous">
</head>
<body>
  <div class="main">
    <p class="main-title" >Django CRUD </p>
      {% block content %}
          {% end block %}
      </div>
  </div>
  <script src="https://code.jquery.com/jquery-3.2.1
.slim.min.js" integrity="sha384-KJ3o2DKtIkvYIK3UE
NzmM7KCkRr/rE9/Qpg6aAZGJwFDMVNA/GpGFF93hXpG5KkN"
crossorigin="anonymous"></script>
  <script src="https://cdnjs.cloudflare.com/ajax/
libs/popper.js/1.12.9/umd/popper.min.js" integrity=
"sha384-ApNbgh9B+Y1QKtv3Rn7W3mgPxhU9K/ScQsAP7hUibX
```

```
39j7fakFPskvXusvfa0b4Q" crossorigin="anonymous"></
script>
  <script src="https://maxcdn.bootstrapcdn.com/
bootstrap/4.0.0/js/bootstrap.min.js" integrity="sha3
84-JZR6Spejh4U02d8jOt6vLEHfe/JQGiRRSQQxSfFWpi1MquV
dAyjUar5+76PVCmYl" crossorigin="anonymous"></
script>
</body>
</html>
```

In base.html, the first step while creating templates for the project is to make the base template. It is used to set the top navigation bar and the footer, and provide the body canvas for any page. Using this base template, we can give a traditional look to our HTML page with any duplicate code. The base.html files can have huge lines of code.

The topline shows that we were commenting on our text like that {# add any text}. The {% load static %} tag is used to add load in the static folder in the base file. This is the critical part of the templating language. It provides you with the specific features of the file that can be changed by pages that extend it. Any page that opens the base.html could easily change the title by writing {% block title %} Add Text {% end block title %}.

Example:

{% include 'navbar.html' %}

Include will help you to extend the page it always writes on top of the code.

{% block content %}

...... In between the block, you can add your HTML code for rendering.

{% end block %}

This helps a lot more to extend your template and reduce the repetition of the common code like style sheets, JavaScript code, etc.

- **templates > Edit.html**

```
{% extends 'base.html' %}
{% block content %}
```

```
<form method="POST" >
  {% csrf_token %}
  <!-- <span>Email</span>  <input type="email"
name="email"> -->
Update your Data:
<input type="text" name="todo" value="{{todo.0.to
dos}}" >
  <!-- {{form}} -->
  <br>
  <button class="btn--primary"> Save </button>
</form>
{% end block %}
```

The project has one edit.html template so that we can update our task in the to-do list. Using the form tag, we can update the value using the name attributes that refer to the model attributes. {{todo.0.todos}} will fetch the value of the user who is authenticated. All the provided code should be written in {% block content%} and don't forget to end this block {% end block%}. With your pressing the save update, the update method will run, and the values are stored instantly when your code is correctly working.

Edit Page

Figure 12.1 shows the edit page.

After Edit Page

Once you have finished editing your data, the old content gets updated (Figure 12.2).

Django CRUD

FIGURE 12.1   Edit you current data.

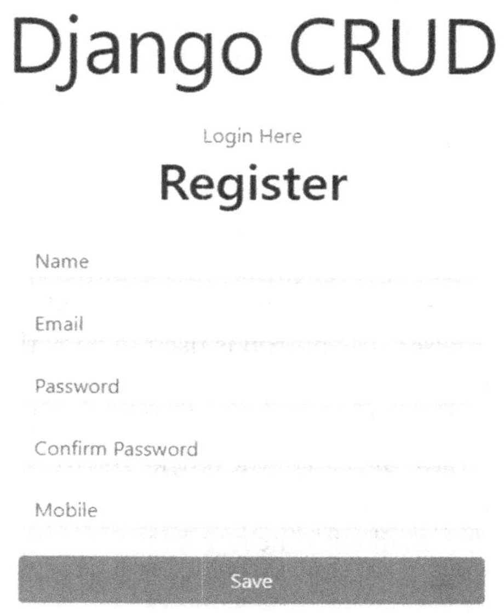

Django CRUD

Login Here

Register

Name

Email

Password

Confirm Password

Mobile

Save

FIGURE 12.2   Updation of data done here.

- **templates > Login.html**

```
{% extends 'base.html' %}
{% block content %}
<a class="links" href="{% url 'register' %}" >
Register Here </a>
<h1> Login </h1>
<form method="POST" >
  {% csrf_token %}
  <!-- <span>Email</span>  <input type="email"
name="email"> -->
  <label>Mobile Number</label>
  <input class="form__field" type="number"
name="number"> <br>
  <label>Password</label>
  <input class="form__field" type="password"
name="password"> <br>
  <button class="btn--primary"> Save </button>
</form>
{% endblock %}
```

The login page will describe the login form for users to enter their login details to access their accounts. {% extends 'base.html' %} extends the code by adding the dependenices.html on top. Next, we have <form> tags with method POST that is secure to store data over the internet. {% csrf_token %} helps to prevent us from the various attack from SQL injection so that nobody can access your site. The form has two input tags which have numbers and passwords. It also has some attributes like number defines the number of the field and if you want to store the data, you can refer to the name to use, the placeholder defines the name which shows inside the input tags on the browser. The button is used to click the event, when you press any button, something will happen. Below the button, we have an anchor tag that mainly works as routing. It will redirect us to the registration page; at last, we have the end of the block. The whole code should be in the block section; otherwise, your legend will not render. In Django form, we are overriding the email with the number.

Login Page

Figure 12.3 shows the login page.

- **templates > register.html**

```
{% extends 'base.html' %}
{% block content %}
<a href="{% url 'login' %}" > Login Here </a>
<h1>Register</h1>
  <form method="POST">
    {% if error %}
```

FIGURE 12.3   User login page.

```
{{error}}
{% endif %}
{% csrf_token %}
<input placeholder="Name" class="form__field"
type="type" name="uname"> <br>
<input placeholder="Email" class="form__field"
type="email" name="email"> <br>
<input placeholder="Password" class="form__
field" type="password" name="password1"> <br>
<input placeholder="Confirm Password"
class="form__field" type="password"
name="password2"> <br>
<input placeholder="Mobile" class="form__field"
type="number" name="number" > <br>
<button class="btn--primary"> Save </button>
</form>
{% end block %}
```

The register page will describe the registration form for users to enter their login details to access their accounts. {% extends 'base.html' %} extends the code by adding the base.html on top. Base.html is the file where we get all the standard code included in every template page. The register form is slightly different from the login page here. We have four input tags: username, email, password, and confirm password. The user has to enter these details. {% csrf_token %} token is required for data storage or retrieval.

Register Page

Figure 12.4 shows the register page.

Django CRUD

123456789   Logout

Add Something

Save

Todo Name   Delete Edit

Hello, my name is Kiran   Delete   Edit

FIGURE 12.4   User registration page.

- **templates > show.html**

```
{%extends 'base.html'%}
{% block content %}
<div class="user">
  <div class="user-name">
    <em>{{A_USER}}</em>
  </div>
  <div class="user-logout">
    <a class="links" href="{% url 'logout'
%}">Logout</a>
  </div>
</div>
  <form method="POST" >
    {% csrf_token %}
    <input class="form__field"
type="text"name="todo" placeholder="Add
Something"><br>
    <button class="btn--primary">Save</button>
  </form>
  <table class="content">
    <tr>
      <th>Todo Name</th>
      <th>Delete</th>
      <th>Edit</th>
    </tr>
    {% for item in get_item %}
    <tr>
      <td>{{item.todos}}</td>
      <td><a class="links" href="{% url 'delete'
item.id %}">Delete</a></td>
      <td><a class="links" href="{% url 'edit' item
.id %}">Edit</a> </td>
    </tr>
    {% endfor %}
  </table>
{% endblock %}
```

Show.html can return to you all the tasks you have stored in your account. Let's have a look over the code. {% extends 'base.html' %} extends the code by adding the base.html on top. Base.html is the file where we get all the common code included in our template page. In <div> tags section,

{{A_USER }} is written which means if yours is authenticated, the name of the user will show here. Besides this code, we have a logout button so that users can log out from their accounts. Every time for navigating the link, always use {% URL 'logout' %}. Then first start with the post method, which have input tags used for storing tasks in the database. The view.py handles all the queries. At last, we have a table with its child tags tr, th, td. Tr is defined as table row, th as table heading, and td as table data. The first row is created, then <th>Todo Name</th>, <th>Delete</th>, <th>Edit</th>, this code will add as it is. Then for loop, run get the To-do data from the database {% for the item in get_item %}, every time a new row will be created. The data from the database is displayed with the help of { {wirte you code here } }. Besides that, two links are there to delete and edit. Delete will delete the selected To-do one at the time and edit goes to the new URL edit.html.

Show Details Page

Figure 12.5 displays the show details page.

Add something to your list and check; your data will be shown instantly when you click the save button (Figure 12.6).

Views.py

```
from django.http.response import
HttpResponseRedirect
from django.shortcuts import redirect, render,
get_list_or_404
from django.http import HttpResponse
from .models import *
```

FIGURE 12.5   Listed all the To-do here.

FIGURE 12.6   To-do created.

```python
from django.contrib import messages
from django.contrib.auth.models import User,auth
from django.contrib.auth import authenticate, logout
from django.contrib.auth.decorators import
login_required
from .forms import *
def login(request):
  if request.method == "POST":
    # Get the value from input
    phone = request.POST.get('number')
    password=request.POST.get('password')
    print(phone, password)
    user_auth = auth.authenticate(username=phone,
password=password)
    print("USER_AUTH" , user_auth)
       if user_auth is not None:
      auth.login(request,user_auth)
      print(user_auth)
      messages.success(request, 'Auth User')
      return redirect('/show')
    else:
      messages.success(request, 'User not found')
      return redirect('/')
  return render(request,'login.html')
def register(request):
  if request.method == "POST":
    if request.POST['password1'] == request.
POST['password2']:
```

```
      try :
        user = User.objects.get(username=request.P
OST['uname'])
        return render(request,'register.html',{'er
ror':"Username Has been Taken"})
      except User.DoesNotExist:
        user = User.objects.create_user(username=r
equest.POST['number'],first_name=request.POST['una
me'],email=request.POST['email'],password = request.
POST['password1'])
        user.save()
        auth.login(request,user)
        return redirect('/')
    else:
      return render(request,'register.html',{'error':
"Password Dose Not Match"})
  else:
    return render(request,'register.html')
@login_required
def show(request):
  A_USER = request.user
  if request.method == "POST":
    todo= request.POST.get('todo')
    print(todo)
    if todo is not None:
      todo_item = TodoModel(todos = todo, user =
request.user)
      todo_item.save()
      # print(todo_item)
  get_todo =TodoModel.objects.filter(user = request
.user)
  return render(request,'show.html',{'get_item':g
et_todo,'A_USER':A_USER})
def logout(request):
  auth.logout(request)
  return redirect('/')
def delete(request,id):
  todo_delete = TodoModel.objects.get(id = id)
  print(todo_delete)
  todo_delete.delete()
  return redirect('/show')
def edit(request,id):
```

```
if request.method =="POST":
  todo = request.POST.get('todo')
  # AUTH USER GET ID
  todo_obj = TodoModel.objects.get(id=id)
  # For storing the value in particular field in
  # in Todo Model 'todos' field.
  todo_obj.todos = todo
  todo_obj.save()
  print("Todo",todo,"TODOS",todo_obj)
  return redirect('/show')
else:
  # Return the particular value with id.
  todo = TodoModel.objects.filter(id=id)
  return render(request,'edit.html',{'todo':todo})
```

1. **view.py is the logic files for the whole Django project:** From Django. shortcuts import redirect, render. This piece of code contains the critical functionality in the project while causing the text to the template and turning to the exact URL to make the site dynamic. You can get all the redirect and return from Django. Shortcuts.

2. **Django.contrib.auth import login, logout, authenticate:** This will help you make your view safe like once the user is registered, only the same user can access the site. Login, logout helps to pass the authenticated user with authentication in the previous chapters; you have learned all the data stored in the admin panel about the admin panel.

3. **From .forms import *:** Form play a vital role here because you can get your form data directly by importing it in the view.py file. Form data can only be stored when the user enters the details and hits the POST method. That is why in every form, we always write if method == POST; this code will only run when the method match.

4. **From .models import *:** The model file import like this when a user enter its data in the form foms.py runs, and data will be saved when the save() method execute, the below code is the example of the save method.

5. **From Django.HTTP import HttpResponse:** HttpResponse returns the text to the client back to the browser. Whenever a request comes

into play, it is handled by the Middleware and rendered by the HttpResponse.

6. **From django.contrib.auth.models import auth:** contrib.auth in your INSTALLED_APP setting.py file will ensure the four default common permission – add, delete, change, and view.

This is the common importing model in the view.py.

All the logic of the Django project should be written in separate functions. We have different functions for each page so that everything looks better and runs in the proper way. Have a look over the code of the home page.

Our first function is about login with the request as a parameter. It will only get implemented when the request method is POST. In the first two lines, when the user enters their number and password in Django, we can get the input like it. print(phone,password) has its own purpose. It is basically used for debugging the code. The user name and password will be shown in the console terminal of the editor. Authentication is the method that checks if a user is present in the User Model. This is Django's default User model, i.e., "user_auth = auth.authenticate(username=phone, password=password)." If the user exists, then the auth. login will run, auth.login(request,user_auth) and if it returns True, the next line executes after the successful login and the message will print with messages. success(request, 'Auth User'). If the user is not found, it redirects the user to the root URL.

The next method is register.html. When it gets the POST method, it will both match and confirm the password. If the password does not match, an error will occur. If both match, the code is moved to a try statement; also try block check, if the user already exists, then a message will appear saying that the username is already taken by somebody, you can add your own message. If the entered name is not found, the except block runs. It will create a new user with email, username, password, and save it in the database, and then authorized user redirects to the next page. If any other error occurs, the user redirects to the same register page.

The show is the third method we have, and this page will only show when the authenticated user is logged in. If the user is a valid user, it will redirect to this page. The page opens on this particular page. The user can add their task list when it is completed, and the user can delete it or edit it any time. This page will not be obtained by anyone because we have used request.user and so will be obtained by the valid user. The authorized user can only get the data here and we have to filter the values of that particular user.

In the logout method, the user logout option is only present. They can log out at any time and when there is a need they can log in. The page will redirect the user to the main page.

The delete() matches the ID of passed object before deletion.

The edit method is also done with the id. We get the id first and then get data from the user input as requested.POST.get('todo'). Next, the id matches and once we get that id and its corresponding todo, the user changes the value and hits the save button; the todo will save in the same place, i.e., override that data and after that page will render to the show itself.

urls.py

```
from django.contrib import admin
from django.urls import path
from .views import *
from django.contrib.staticfiles.urls import
staticfiles_urlpatterns
urlpatterns = [
  path('',login,name="login"),
  path('register',register,name="register"),
  path('show',show,name="show"),
  path('logout',logout,name="logout"),
  path('delete/<id>',delete,name="delete"),
  path('edit/<id>',edit,name="edit"),
]
```

1. From Django.contrib import admin

   It automatically looks for an admin module in each application and imports them.

2. From Django.URLs import path

   The path function contains the Django.URL module. It is used for routing URLs to the appropriate view function within an application using dispatcher (expression).

3. From Django.URLs.conf import

   A function that takes full import path to another URLconf module where include can be added. The dot (.) operator is shorthand for the current package.

4. From quiz app.URLs import *

   quiz app.URLs are the URL file of the quiz app application, so here we are just importing them to use them.

5. From Django.contrib.staticfiles.URLs import staticfiles_urlpatterns – This will return the URL pattern for serving static files already defined in the pattern list.

6. URL patterns – It refers to the mapping of URLs to function name and views the first parameter for adding the URLs, then next is about the view function name. This method should be the same as defined in the view.py.

model.py

In the code shown below, we imported the model from Django.db. It is a built-in module with various packages that we can use in our project. The database tables are created through the help of the class keyword in "model.py".

```
# Create your tests here.
#https://testdriven.io/blog/django-custom-user
-model/
from django.db import models
from django.contrib.auth.models import User
class TodoModel(models.Model):
  user = models.ForeignKey(User,on_delete=models.
CASCADE,null=True)
  todos = models.CharField(max_length=20 ,
blank=True)
  def __str__(self):
    return f"User {self.user}"
```

These fields are of the model's name TodoModel having user fields as Foreign Key, which is a column in a table whose values must match values in some other table, meaning the fields user of TodoModel now has the same value as the User model which is the Django's inbuilt model. Whenever we delete this user, all the data related to this user will be deleted.

On_delete – It tells Django what to do with the model's field that depends on the model instance you have deleted. CASCADE tells Django to cascade the deleting effect. This constraint in MYSQL is to delete the row from the table when the rows from the parent are deleted. Every field must have a Field type like above. We have CharField(). It is a text-based column and accepts "max_length" of 200 characters and in our next fields, todos have max_length of only 20 characters, blank=True means by default this field is blank.

__str__(): It tells Django what to print. It returns the string representation of the object of the model. F string (f"") is a way of embedding an expression inside the literal string; you can use the quotes, double or even triple, to create your literal string. For evaluating the expression in f string, write it into the {} curly braces like {self. user}. Here, self is for pointing to the current user name.

forms.py

```
from Django. forms import fields
from .models import TodoModel
from Django import forms
from Django.contrib.auth import models
class TodoForm(forms.Form):
    todos = forms.CharField( max_length=100)
class UpdateForm(forms.ModelForm):
    class Meta:
      model = TodoModel
      fields = ['todos']
      widgets = {
        'todos':forms.TextInput(attrs={
          'class':'form__field'
        })
      }
```

We have some importing fields in this form.py:

1. **From Django.forms import fields:** This field is used in the class Meta as fields = ['todos']. It will return all the fields of the todo model of TodoForm.

2. **From .models import TodoModel:** We import the defined models on the TodoModel of the model.py.

3. **From Django import forms:** Here, we get access to our defined form. With this line of code, we can import the form in model.py. Form can be used directly in the template as {{ form }}.

4. **From Django.contrib.auth import models:** This code import the models from Django.contrib listed in setting.py in the portion of INSTALLED_APPS = [ ]. For the user default model, the user identifier is the username.

```
INSTALLED_APPS = [
  'django.contrib.auth',
]
```

UpdateForm is the class that consists of the Meta class: We can customize data as per our needs, like we can use the same model in the UpdateForm. Widgets are for adding customization in the forms.

Apps.py

```
from Django. apps import AppConfig
class TodoConfig(AppConfig):
  default_auto_field = 'django.db.models.BigAutoF
ield'
  name = 'Todo'
```

It is a configuration that is common to all Django applications. The AppConfig used to configure the application has a path attribute. BigAutoField is an auto-incrementing primary key according to the available IDs like AutoField.

admin.py

Let's move to "admin.py" and do an import of the models called TodoModel by using "from .models import TodoModel".

```
# Register your models here.
from Django.contrib import admin
from .models import *
admin.site.register(TodoModel)
```

In admin.py

Static > myfile.css

```css
body {
  padding: 0;
  margin: 0;
    box-sizing: border-box;
}
  .main {
  width:100vh;
  margin:0 auto;
  height: 100vh;
  display: flex;
      flex-direction: column;
      justify-content: center;
      align-items: center;
}
  .main-title {
  font-size: 10vh;
}
form{
  display: flex;
  flex-direction: column;
}
.form__field {
  width: 360px;
  background: #fff;
  color: #a3a3a3;
  font: inherit;
  box-shadow: 0 6px 10px 0 rgba(0, 0, 0 , .1);
  border: 0;
  outline: 0;
  padding: 1px 12px;
}
label {
  width: 50%;
}
form{
  margin:20px;
}
li{
    width: 120px;
```

```
  }
  .btn {
   display: inline-block;
   background: transparent;
   color: inherit;
   font: inherit;
   border: 0;
   outline: 0;
   padding: 0;
   transition: all 200ms ease-in;
   cursor: pointer;
  }
  .user{
   width:50%;
   display: flex;
   flex-direction: row;
   justify-content: space-between;
  }
  table {
   display: flex;
   flex-direction: column;
   justify-content: space-evenly;
   align-items: center;
   font-family: arial, sans-serif;
   border-collapse: collapse;
  }
  td, th {
   border: 1px solid #dddddd;
   text-align: left;
   padding: 8px;
  }
  tr:nth-child(even) {
   background-color: #dddddd;
  }
.links{
 color:#7f8ff4;
}
.links:hover{
 color: rgb(0, 0, 0);
 text-decoration: none;
}
.btn--primary {
```

```
background:#7f8ff4;
color:#fff;
box-shadow: 0 0 10px 2px rgba(0, 0, 0, .1);
border-radius: 2px;
padding: 12px 16px;
    }
```

In this file, we have done our styling part, and this file should be in a static folder.

Comparative Study between Django, Flask, Node.Js, and Spring Boot

IN THIS CHAPTER

➢ Introduction about frameworks

➢ Comparison with Flask

➢ Comparison with Node.Js

➢ Comparison with Spring Boot

Here you will learn the difference between the most popular and in-demand Python-based frameworks.

Python is an advanced programming language used in data science, developing websites and software, automating tasks, building control and management, and testing. Many non-programmers have adopted it for everday tasks. There are many Python frameworks.

Its frameworks offer well-defined structures for app development. They can automate and carry through some standard solutions.

DOI: 10.1201/9781003310495-13

Django.

TYPES OF PYTHON FRAMEWORK

Python frameworks are categorized into various types:

1. **Full Stack Framework**: Also known as enterprise framework, it is one of the best solutions for all development needs. It is a person who can quickly develop both client and server-side software. These have built-in libraries to work smoothly and continuously. They hold up the development of databases, frontend interfaces, and backend services. The Full Stack developer can handle all the benefits.

2. **Micro Framework**: These frameworks are lightweight, minimalistic web applications that limit functionalities and features. They are required for just building an application. They lack additional functionality like control database stuff, authentication, validation, and backend services.

Let's have a look at the difference between the Python frameworks.

WHAT IS FLASK?

It is an API of Python that allows us to build up web applications. Armin Ronacher developed it, and it is easier to learn because it has less code to implement. A Web Application Framework is the collection of modules and libraries that helps the developer to write applications. It is based on the WSGI (Web Server Gateway Interface) toolkit and Jinja2 templates.

Comparison of Flask with Django.

Let's have a look at how they compare to Django:

1. Django is a full-stack web framework that enables ready-to-use with its batteries-included approach. Flask is a lightweight micro-framework that gives abundant features without eternal libraries and minimalist elements.

2. Django provides its own Django ORM (object-relational-mapper) and uses data models, while Flask doesn't have any data model. Django bundles everything, whereas Flask is more modular.

3. Django has a massive number of built packages, whereas Flask has minimalistic packages.

4. The admin interface is what makes Django a capable web system, whereas this is not true for Flask.

5. Django is convenient for more significant projects that need a lot of functionality. For simple projects, the features can be consuming more space.

6. Django needs two more lines of code than Flask, where Flask applications require much fewer lines of code for simple tasks.

7. The Django tools are built-in tools with which developers can build a web application without external. Admin features are not as well-known as in Django.

8. Django has a vast and active developer community. Whenever you have any questions about any topic, you can ask them on various platforms like web portals, where Flask has not the big community as Django.

9. Django can easily protect its application from these issues.

   - Cross-site scripting (XSS): It enables an attacker to inject the client-side scripts into browsers. Django protects its application from these attacks.

   - Cross-site request forgery (CSRF): CSRF attacks allow the invalid user to execute their action using another user's credentials.

   - SQL injection: It is an attack where the user can execute the SQL code on a database.

Where Flask library provides the same, Django also prevents the data from significant loss and other web attacks.

10. Django separates the routes from the function, where Flask uses decorators on the function to set routes.

11. Django has so many third-party libraries and packages. That's why it is not easy to learn whereas Flask has none these features. It is easy to understand.

Basic Comparison	Django	Flask
Structure	It is a Python-based free, open-source framework that follows the MTV structure pattern because the controller is handled by the framework itself. Some of the functionality is done by models, templates, and views. It is considered a Full Stack Framework	It is a Python-based micro-framework for any set of particular tools or external libraries. It also doesn't have a database layer or provisions for form validation and makes use of extensions
Features	• ORM (object-relational-mapper) • View – web templating • Model – relational • Caching • Inheritance • Controller – regex-based URL dispatcher • Middleware classes support • Internationalization • Unit-testing framework • Authentication • Admin interface • Atom and RSS syndication feeds • Google's sitemaps • Framework for GIS applications • Extensibility • Server arrangements	Development server Development debugger Inbuilt support for unit Jinja2 templates RESTful request dispatch Support for secure cookies Full WSGI complaint Extensive Documentation High flexibility Easily deployable in production ORM – agnostic
Project Layout	Conventional project structure	Arbitrary structure
Sites using these frameworks	Public Broadcasting Service, Mozilla, Instagram, Nextdoor	Pinterest, LinkedIn, Flask community
Flexibility	It doesn't exclude setting flexibility	It is believed that all possible permutations that organize a Flask code equal the application number present in the Flask already

(Continued)

Basic Comparison	Django	Flask
Routing	Url.py is used to set the connection properties, and the request is tackled by the first matching view of the regex list	URL is most frequently used than not set by the view decorator, and centralized configuration is also possible
Advantages	Lots of batteries Huge third party Functional admin panel Versioning Browsable API Descriptive and elaborative	Speed Support for NoSQL Minimal complexity No ORM, easily connected with extensions
Templates	It helps you to utilize the View web templating	Uses a Ninja2 templates design
Working style	It offers a diversified working style	It offers a monolithic working style
URL dispatcher	Based on controller-regex	Based on RESTful request
HTML features	Offers HTML	Does not offer HTML
Visual Debug	No support for Visual Debug	Support for Visual Debug
Third-party application	Support for third-party application	Does not support third-party application
API	Does not support	Support AAI
Databases	Doesn't support multiple databases	Support multiple databases

DJANGO VS NODE.JS

What Is Node.js?

It is an open-source and cross-platform runtime environment for executing JavaScript code. Node.js is not a framework, and it's not a programming language. Node.js for building backend services such as like APIs and Mobile App. It is used by large production companies such as PayPal, Uber, and Walmart.

Node.js with Django.

Let's have a look at how Node.Js compares to Django.

1. **Definitions**: The difference between Django and Node.js is that node is an open-source system that runs on JavaScript. It is intended for a developer whose intention is to build a robust application interface. It is an open-source, free Python-based structure for expert developers whose point is to build PC applications.

2. **Community**: The difference between both is that Node.JS has quite an active community with experienced clients to help you with the updates, while Django has a small community compared to Node.Js.

3. **Efficiency**: Node.Js structure is not difficult to adapt, whereas Django is more effective and offers quick speed.

4. **Security**: Node.Js is not just as secure as Django and requires manual activities in the framework to manage security, while Django is more secure.

Basic Comparison	Django	Node
Definitions	It is an open-source web framework	It is an open-source and JS run-time environment
Programmed	It was programmed in Python	It was written in C, C++, and JavaScript
Scalable	It is less scalable	It is more scalable comparatively
Performance	Its performance is better	Its performance is good
Architecture	It follows the model template view architecture for purposes of handling data, validating, and interacting	It follows event-driven programming. Run on many operating systems, and maintain a small list of requests
Complexity	It is more complex for the developers to follow a predefined path to solve the problem	It is less complicated than Django. The developer has the freedom to operate in their way
Official Website	https://www.djangoproject.com/	https://nodejs.org/en/
Leading	It is new and behind Node.js in usage	It is used widely in many countries and ahead comparatively
Security	High	Medium

(Continued)

Basic Comparison	Django	Node
Rapid development	Most recommended	Recommended
Architecture	Model View Template structure with a web framework	Single thread event loop with a run-time environment
Cost-efficiency	It is more energetic and gives fast speed, making it more cost-powerful	It is much safe to learn but absorbs more functioning time, making it also a cost-effective alternative
Flexibility	It provides definite flexibility and has to serve development features	With the JavaScript library, several tools and features are available in Node.Js. You can even make a JS-based app from scratch
Reputation	It has a good and solid reputation	Its popularity is growing with time. Some becomes a preferred framework
Development speed	Less operating time due to built-in system, time-consuming in learning if developers don't know Python	More operating time but helpful if developers are influential and if the developers are experienced with JavaScript
Tool type	Web environment	Runtime framework

DJANGO VS. SPRING BOOT

What Is Spring Boot?

It is a well-known Java framework for creating business applications. It's a web-based application with a strong point of view. It enables you to quickly launch a product, a stand-alone application. It's written in Java, and the concept behind the SR is to make things simple. It diminishes the amount of effort required to get an application up and running. It provides you with the dependency separation feature and so on.

Comparison of Spring Root with Django.

Some Sprint Boot features:

- It allows for quick web application creation.

- Some embedded servers are valuable to execute the applications.

- It allows you to operate with a similar application in various content by using a YAML file.

- It ensures that the apps are secure.

- It depends on annotations and XML files. Sprint boot makes it simple to get started with the project.

Let's have a look at how the Spring Boot Java-based framework compares to the Python-based framework used in Django.

Django	String Boot
It's free, open-source, and easy to learn	It's free, open-source.
It is a Python-based web development framework	It is a Java-based web development framework
Less complex than Spring Boot, Django is popular	The spring is a Java-based framework, and it may be challenging to understand
It also offers web development in a rush	It provides the facility for the creation of Java projects fast
It is more challenging to set up than the Spring Boot environment	Setting up and spring a project using SB is simple
It has a large community	It has a small community as compared to Django
It provides a full-text search	There is no notion of full-text search in it

After comparing the rest of the framework with Django, what we have learned is that every framework has its features. Some frameworks are suitable for small development, some for large. They allow the developer to use modules for faster growth. So choose your framework wisely.

CHAPTER SUMMARY

In this chapter, you learned about the difference between the Python-based framework Django and Flask, Node.Js, and Spring Boot. Django has various features that Flask, Node.Js, and Spring Boot don't have. Every framework has pros and cons. It is up to you to chose which one you are going to use.

Appraisal

IF YOU WANT TO be a full-stack developer, this book will help you to do so from scratch. At present, the development is at a peak. You may have seen that many big companies have started their work from scratch with the development of new technologies. They all learn and implement technologies in their products. The fundamentals of full-stack development skills include web technologies like HTML, CSS, and JavaScript as well as databases, frameworks, and many more. Now you can extend their functionality by using third-party packages. The world of technology is constantly changing, and with periods of growing demand and a need for technologies to provide effective code products, new technologies are frequently introduced by various companies. Why do you want to be full-stack developer? What is important to know about it?

Full-stack developers know multiple technologies like frontend and backend technologies. They are familiar with all of them. There is no compulsion that you should be suitable for full stack only. You can go for either the frontend (client side) or the backend (server side). Technical skills for frontend developers include HTML, CSS, JavaScript, and important aspects of frontend development like user experience, some validations, and responsiveness. They must be familiar with at least one frontend framework like Angular.js, React, Vue.js, JQuery, and so on. Knowing about the framework will also enhance your chance to get a good job globally. Once they get command over the frontend, they can go further to the backend. The skills required for backend development are the knowledge of at least one of backend language (PHP, Java, C#, Ruby,.Net, Python) and experience with database and server configuration and APIs. Database layer management is also a part of full stack. They must work with some basic queries like storing, creating, and managing the data from the server, whether cloud-based or locally installed. Popular full-stack development includes LAMP Stack, MEAN STACK, MERN STACK, PHP Full Stack, Python Full Stack, Java Full Stack, and Django Full Stack. Many people have already chosen full-stack development as a career and many more will do so in the future. It is in high demand due to its vast development. The career is open to you when you get into it. You can go for anything and also change your path by learning new things. There are built-dynamic, innovative software that provide insights on continuous improvement and remove functionality as per their needs; they can also handle teams of developers and communicate well with them.

What roles do they develop? The full-stack developer usually ends up with variety when they go for a job in frontend fundamentals (as we discussed above), server-side fundamentals, and user experience design, i.e., when designing an application, it is essential to consider only the client's point of view. Therefore, the full-stack developer must have the ability to design UX components. Database architecture and design, i.e., knowing the database, is a must for such a developer. How will the database be structured? How is deployment to be done? – business logic, i.e., the developer must structure the code from the business point of view. Project management is another skill that allows you to enhance the level of your job in full stack. Multitasking, i.e., full stack, will find them dealing with multiple tasks at once while learning the job. There will be more options apart from full-stack development. If you feel comfortable, you can go for it, but you should have a similar skillset. A fundamental fact for this approach is that they are highly skilled in one or more areas, not in everything. They have a general idea of all relevant technologies. Sometimes solo development makes it difficult to handle; having a good team leader can upgrade your skillset.

How to become a Full-Stack Developer? Read the above carefully, and you surely will get a good idea of where to start your developer journey. First, you will have to gather a few years of professional training in some of the reputed companies in order to learn the technologies. You can't be a full-stack developer only with learning. Get some practical knowledge. It's all about constantly learning and getting experience in the frontend as well as backend development.

There are many kinds of resources and courses available to learn about full-stack web development. But always ask yourself what you want to become and in which profession you will get a good guide.

This is what full-stack development is all about. Now let's talk about the most popular Python-based framework – Django.

In this book, we provided you with knowledge on Django and Python. Python is high-level, object-oriented with dynamic semantic. In the beginning, you will face problems with their syntax. If you are a beginner, after getting more deeply into it, it will become easier. Its syntax is very clean, simple, and easy to understand. Most of the companies are working on it. It will provide you more features while working with different frameworks like Django, Flask, etc. Many opportunities will open up for you once you have a good command over Python, for example, Artificial Intelligence, Machine Learning, Mobile application, Web Application development, etc.

Every new field has a different skillset like Python, R, Java, C++ for Artificial Intelligence, as in Machine Learning. Python is open-source, freely available over the internet.

You can perform Django coding in any text editor. It is familiar to everyone, but our recommendation is to do with the ext editor. VS Code (Visual Studio Code) is free and open-source, published by Microsoft. It is also available for Windows, Linux, and macOS. It includes many powerful features that have made it the most popular development tool currently available. Its screen is divided into five regions: the activity bar, the sidebar, editor groups, the panel, and the status bar. This editor has built-in features like you can install Bootstrap directly without downloading manually. For the beginner, this text editor is very handy.

This book is all about Django, its architecture, how it works, how the code runs, how to install a third-party package, and so on. It has various features like increasing the speed and performance of your applications and a batteries-included framework. It provides you with predefined code such as database, session management, HTML templates, and URL routing. It follows the principle of DRY, i.e., Don't Repeat Yourself. The code of every file is reusable in another file. It is a bug-free framework error, and when there is an error in the code, it will be highlighted. To take care of indentation is most important because it is in the Python-based framework that you need to indent your code correctly. We also have numerous options for the package like Django rest framework, Django Allauth, Django shop, cartridge, etc.

Companies like Instagram, Mozilla Firefox, Pinterest, and even NASA are using Django frameworks. Django uses the templating engine Jinja for content displaying. It uses an admin panel for any language. This framework is the extensible framework. Django supports MTV patterns instead of MCV. The controller takes care of the Django itself. We need to focus on models, views, and templates. It is suitable for both the small and large businesses. It supports both SQL and NoSQL databases, making them choose more straightforward small business answers from a wide range of databases. It works on an ORM system, which means it bridges the gap between the data model and database engines. Small businesses can benefit from the ORM system to use relational database management systems like MySQL, Oracle, PostgreSQL, and No SQL databases like MongoDB and Google App Engine. Django and Python are considered portable. You can be ported to many platforms, from PC and Linux to any PlayStation. There are overall 40,000 packages for Django to cover testing debugging. It is secure and up-to-date.

By using this framework, your time will be saved. You won't have to spend hours to code on it. It entirely follows Python, and the Python community is enormous. You can get any code over the internet. You can also get them from their official documentation. Once you feel comfortable with it, you can use it extensively. It is the most popular framework these days. It has its REST framework for building APIs.

This book covered topics like model, view, and template. First, you had a brief introduction to the Python language. You should be aware of Python fundamentals and syntax and how to write things in the Python language. Installation was also covered in this book, and then you learned about requirements for doing projects. We also covered some critical installations like pip. Don't get confused, it's just a part of the installation. Then we looked at Django file structure like where to write a chunk of code so that you have some knowledge of the file and what this file is used for, which means the logical part, database part, and presentation part. In Chapter 4 we learned about syntax, which file takes care of this code (model.py), how to write everything, when to migrate your model in database, etc.

Chapter 5 is based on views. Views are used to write the logical part. Every kind of logic should be written in this file. The next chapter examined templating in Django. Here we use the Jinja template as a templating engine. This template is very handy to make the syntax clear; we quickly get to know what is going on in this template file. In the admin panel, you will see what was stored when you migrated the model. This is used for storing the database from our defined model. We can check and update the model fields as well. Chapter 8 told you about the proper implementation of forms in the template or model files. The entire chapter contains built-in features like their method and function. It makes working easier. In Chapter 9, the advanced quality of the model was defined with their inbuilt Python method. Deployment was reviewed in Chapter 10. We covered the Django deployment with Microsoft Azure, AWS Elastic Bean Stack, and Git with brief information. In Chapter 11, we have a simple project on the Todo list project using Python and Django frameworks with features and functionality like its simple CRUD operation to authenticate where users can store and get their data anytime. We also covered more projects like Quiz App in Django. It will help you know where to start your project and help in the future to get things done more quickly. We also covered the comparative studies of Django with the rest of the framework, like Flask is based on Python, Node.Js is based on JavaScript, and Spring Boot is based on Java. After reading the entire book, beginner and intermediate developers will have more information about Python and Django. Try to do small projects to get more chances to get a good job. You should have hands-on experience with both Python and Django. Many opportunities will open up when you actually know what you want to be in the future, whether you wish to be a full-stack, frontend, or back-end developer. Also, try to remain up-to-date about the latest technologies in the IT fields.

Bibliography

*args and **kwargs in Python.* (2017, May 30). GeeksforGeeks. https://www.geeks-forgeeks.org/args-kwargs-python/

8 Reasons Why Django Web Framework is Best for Web Development. (2021, November 15). Monocubed. https://www.monocubed.com/blog/django-web-framework/

9 Factors to Consider When Choosing a Web Host. (2018, November 12). Cuelogic Technologies Pvt. Ltd. https://www.cuelogic.com/blog/9-factors-to-consider-when-choosing-a-web-host

Acsany, P. (2022, February 2). *Using Python's Pip to Manage Your Projects' Dependencies.* Real Python. https://realpython.com/what-is-pip/

adrianhall. (2022, May 9). *About Azure Mobile Apps.* Microsoft Docs. https://docs.microsoft.com/en-in/azure/developer/mobile-apps/azure-mobile-apps/overview

Banerjee, R. (2021, March 23). *Dunder/Magic Methods in Python. Engineering Education (EngEd) Program.* Section. https://www.section.io/engineering-education/dunder-methods-python/#:~:text=Dunder%20methods%20are%20names%20that,in%20functions%20for%20custom%20classes

Baysan. (2021, November 26). *From Zero to Hero Django Admin: ModelAdmin Class (Part2).* Nerd For Tech | Medium. https://medium.com/nerd-for-tech/from-zero-to-hero-django-admin-modeladmin-class-part2-2c8665d6cd5

Bledsoe, E. (2021, June 30). *Cloud IDE vs Local IDE: Understanding the Differences.* Coder. https://coder.com/blog/cloud-ide-vs-local-ide-understanding-the-differences

Change Object Display Name using __str__ function - Django Models | Python. (2019, October 28). GeeksforGeeks. https://www.geeksforgeeks.org/change-object-display-name-using-__str__-function-django-models-python/#:~:text=str%20function%20in%20a%20django,of%20instances%20for%20that%20model.&text=%23%20Create%20your%20models%20here.,-class%20GeeksModel(Model&text=This%20will%20display%20the%20objects,could%20understand%20using%20self%20object

Chapter 3: Views and URLconfs. (n.d.). Django Book 0.1 Documentation. Retrieved July 10, 2022, from https://django-book.readthedocs.io/en/latest/chapter03.html

Class Based Generic Views Django (Create, Retrieve, Update, Delete. (2020, January 22). GeeksforGeeks. https://www.geeksforgeeks.org/class-based -generic-views-django-create-retrieve-update-delete/

Contributor, T. T. (2012, June 1). *What is Cloud IDE? - Definition from WhatIs .com.* SearchCloudComputing. https://www.techtarget.com/searchcloud computing/definition/cloud-IDE

Crispy Filter. (n.d.). Django-Crispy-Forms 1.14.0 Documentation. Retrieved July 10, 2022, from https://django-crispy-forms.readthedocs.io/en/latest/filters .html

Daityari, S. (2019, May 28). *What's the Best Cloud IDE in 2022? Here Are 8 of the Top Options.* CodeinWP. https://www.codeinwp.com/blog/best-cloud-ide/

Data Flair. (n.d.). Django Exceptions & Error-Handling Made Easy with this Handy Guide! Retrieved July 10, 2022, from https://data-flair.training/ blogs/django-exceptions-and-error-handling/

Deepali. (2021, December 17). *Top Django Interview Questions and Answers for 2022* https://www.naukri.com/learning/articles/django-interview-ques-tions-and-answers/

Deploy a Django App on App Platform. (n.d.). DigitalOcean Documentation. Retrieved July 10, 2022, from https://docs.digitalocean.com/tutorials/app -deploy-django-app/#:~:text=Django%20is%20a%20powerful%20web,and %20an%20extensible%20plugin%20architecture

Difference Between Class-Based Views and Function-Based Views. (n.d.). Javatpoint. Retrieved July 10, 2022, from https://www.javatpoint.com/class -based-views-vs-function-based-views

Django Admin Custom Page Layout, Data & Behaviors. (n.d.). Web Forefront. Retrieved July 10, 2022, from https://www.webforefront.com/django/ admincustomlayout.html

Django Database Connectitvity. (n.d.). Javatpoint. Retrieved July 10, 2022, from https://www.javatpoint.com/django-database-connectitvity

Django Deploy on Github. (n.d.). Javatpoint. Retrieved July 10, 2022, from https:// www.javatpoint.com/django-deploy-on-github

Django Exceptions. (n.d.). Django Documentation | Django. Retrieved July 10, 2022, from https://docs.djangoproject.com/en/4.0/ref/exceptions/

Django Introduction. (2022, April 26). Learn Web Development | MDN. https:// developer.mozilla.org/en-US/docs/Learn/Server-side/Django/Introduction

Django Introduction | Set 2 (Creating a Project). (2018, February 1). GeeksforGeeks. https://www.geeksforgeeks.org/django-introduction-set-2-creating-a -project/

Django Model Data Types and Fields List. (2019, October 3). GeeksforGeeks. https://www.geeksforgeeks.org/django-model-data-types-and-fields-list/

Django ModelForms. (n.d.). Javatpoint. Retrieved July 10, 2022, from https://www .javatpoint.com/django-modelforms

Django Models. (2019, December 20). GeeksforGeeks. https://www.geeksforgeeks .org/django-models/

Django Static Files Handling. (n.d.). Javatpoint. Retrieved July 10, 2022, from https://www.javatpoint.com/django-static-files-handling

Django Template. (n.d.). Javatpoint. Retrieved July 9, 2022, from https://www .javatpoint.com/django-template#:~:text=Django%20Templates,dynamic %20content%20will%20be%20inserted

Django Template. (n.d.). Javatpoint. Retrieved July 10, 2022, from https://www .javatpoint.com/django-template

Django Tutorial Part 11: Deploying Django to Production. (2022, April 28). Learn Web Development, MDN. https://developer.mozilla.org/en-US/docs/Learn /Server-side/Django/Deployment

Django Tutorial Part 3: Using Models. (2022, April 27). Learn Web Development | MDN. https://developer.mozilla.org/en-US/docs/Learn/Server-side/Django /Models

Django Tutorial Part 4: Django Admin Site. (2022, April 7). Learn Web Development | MDN. https://developer.mozilla.org/en-US/docs/Learn/ Server-side/Django/Admin_site

Django Tutorial Part 6: Generic List and Detail Views. (2022, May 23). Learn Web Development | MDN. https://developer.mozilla.org/en-US/docs/Learn/ Server-side/Django/Generic_views

Django URL Mapping. (n.d.). Javatpoint. Retrieved July 10, 2022, from https:// www.javatpoint.com/django-url-mapping

Django UserCreationForm | Creating New User. (n.d.). Javatpoint. Retrieved July 10, 2022, from https://www.javatpoint.com/django-usercreationform

Django vs. Node JS | Difference between Django and Node JS. (n.d.). Javatpoint. Retrieved July 10, 2022, from https://www.javatpoint.com/django-vs -node-js#:~:text=Django%20is%20Python%20based%20web,APIs %20(Client%2Dside).&text=It%20provides%20strong%20security%20 and,system%20which%20prevents%20any%20deficiency

Django.Contrib.Auth. (n.d.). Django Documentation | Django. Retrieved July 10, 2022, from https://docs.djangoproject.com/en/4.0/ref/contrib/auth/

Django.Urls Functions for Use in URLconfs. (n.d.). Django Documentation | Django. Retrieved July 10, 2022, from https://docs.djangoproject.com/en/4 .0/ref/urls/

Django-Babel. (2017, December 18). PyPI. https://pypi.org/project/django -babel/#:~:text=Babel%20provides%20a%20message%20extraction,extrac- tion%20functionality%20is%20rather%20limited

Dugar, D. (2020, April 25). *Jinja2 Explained in 5 Minutes!. (Part 4: Back-End Web Framework: Flask).* Medium. https://codeburst.io/jinja-2-explained-in-5 -minutes-88548486834e

Exploring Project Structure & Creating Django App. (2021, April 9). PyCharm Guide. https://www.jetbrains.com/pycharm/guide/tutorials/django-aws/ project-explore/

FileMaker Pro 18 Advanced Help. (n.d.). FileMaker. Retrieved July 10, 2022, from https://fmhelp.filemaker.com/help/18/fmp/en/index.html#page/FMP_Help /one-to-one-relationships.html

Flask vs Django. (n.d.). Javatpoint. Retrieved July 10, 2022, from https://www .javatpoint.com/flask-vs-django#:~:text=Both%20Django%20and%20Flask %20are,lightweight%20and%20extensible%20web%20framework

Flask vs Django - Javatpoint. (n.d.). Javatpoint. Retrieved July 10, 2022, from https://www.javatpoint.com/flask-vs-django#:~:text=Both%20Django %20and%20Flask%20are,lightweight%20and%20extensible%20web %20framework

Form Assets (The Media Class). (n.d.). Django Documentation | Django. Retrieved July 10, 2022, from https://docs.djangoproject.com/en/4.0/topics/forms/ media/

General Python FAQ. (n.d.). Python 3.10.5 Documentation. Retrieved July 9, 2022, from https://docs.python.org/3/faq/general.html#:~:text=Finally %2C%20Python%20is%20portable%3A%20it,and%20macOS%2C%20and %20on%20Windows

How Much Python Should You know to Learn Django? (2021, March 27). GeeksforGeeks. https://www.geeksforgeeks.org/how-much-python-should -you-know-to-learn-django/#:~:text=It's%20not%20easy%20to%20 learn,object%2Doriented%20programming%20in%20Python

How to Deploy Django. (n.d.). Django 4.0.6 Documentation. Retrieved July 10, 2022, from https://django.readthedocs.io/en/stable/howto/deployment/ index.html

How to Install Django on Windows. (n.d.). Django Documentation | Django. Retrieved July 9, 2022, from https://docs.djangoproject.com/en/1.8/howto /windows/#:~:text=Django%20can%20be%20installed%20easily,version %20in%20the%20command%20prompt

How to Install Python in Windows? (n.d.). Tutorialspoint. Retrieved July 9, 2022, from https://www.tutorialspoint.com/how-to-install-python-in-windows

How to Perform URL Routing in Django. (n.d.). Educative: Interactive Courses for Software Developers. Retrieved July 10, 2022, from https://www.educative .io/answers/how-to-perform-url-routing-in-django

HTTP Status Codes Glossary. (2022, July 5). WebFX. https://www.webfx.com/ web-development/glossary/http-status-codes/

https://www.sciencedirect.com/topics/computer-science/interpreted-lan- guage#:~:text=Python%20is%20an%20interpreted%20language,like %20code%20for%20these%20languages.

Integrated Development Environment. (2018, October 10). Wikipedia. https://en .wikipedia.org/wiki/Integrated_development_environment#:~:text=An %20integrated%20development%20environment%20(IDE,automation%20 tools%20and%20a%20debugger (last edited on September 1, 2022).

Introduction to AWS Elastic Beanstalk. (2020, May 26). GeeksforGeeks. https:// www.geeksforgeeks.org/introduction-to-aws-elastic-beanstalk/

Jaysha. (2021, April 21). Ordinary Coders. https://ordinarycoders.com/blog/arti- cle/render-a-django-form-with-bootstrap

Joy, A. (2020, February 11). *How to Change the Default Runserver Port in Django.* Pythonista Planet. https://pythonistaplanet.com/how-to-change-the -default-runserver-port-in-django/

Lutz, M. (2013, June 1). *Learning Python,* 5th ed. O'Reilly Online Learning. https:// www.oreilly.com/library/view/learning-python-5th/9781449355722/

Managing Files. (n.d.). Django Documentation | Django. Retrieved July 10, 2022, from https://docs.djangoproject.com/en/4.0/topics/files/

Many-to-One Relationships. (n.d.). Django Documentation | Django. Retrieved July 10, 2022, from https://docs.djangoproject.com/en/4.0/topics/db/examples/many_to_one/

Matosevic, M. (2022, March 9). *How to Check Django Version?* ZeroToByte. https://zerotobyte.com/how-to-check-django-version/

Memory Management in Python. (2020, April 30). GeeksforGeeks. https://www.geeksforgeeks.org/memory-management-in-python/#:~:text=Memory%20allocation%20can%20be%20defined,to%20do%20manual%20garbage%20collection

Middleware. (n.d.). Django Documentation | Django. Retrieved July 10, 2022, from https://docs.djangoproject.com/en/1.8/topics/http/middleware/

Mitchel, J. (2018, March 8). *How Django URLs Work with Regular Expressions.* Coding for Entrepreneurs. https://www.codingforentrepreneurs.com/blog/how-django-urls-work-with-regular-expressions/#:~:text=We%20use%20regular%20expressions%20to,404%20Page%20Not%20Found%20response

Model Field Reference. (n.d.). Django Documentation | Django. Retrieved July 10, 2022, from https://docs.djangoproject.com/en/4.0/ref/models/fields/

Model View Controller (MVC) and Link with Django (MTV). (2020, June 12). OpenGenus IQ: Computing Expertise & Legacy. https://iq.opengenus.org/model-view-controller-django/

More, R., & About. (2016, July 17). *How to Create a Custom Django Middleware.* Simple Is Better Than Complex. https://simpleisbetterthancomplex.com/tutorial/2016/07/18/how-to-create-a-custom-django-middleware.html

One-to-Many or Many-to-One Relationship in DBMS. (n.d.). Tutorialspoint. Retrieved July 10, 2022, from https://www.tutorialspoint.com/One-to-Many-or-Many-to-One-Relationship-in-DBMS

Python (Programming Language). (1991, February 20). Wikipedia. https://en.wikipedia.org/wiki/Python_(programming_language) (last edited on September 6, 2022).

Python Built-in Functions. (n.d.). Tutorialsteacher. Retrieved July 10, 2022, from https://www.tutorialsteacher.com/python/builtin-methods

Python, R. (n.d.). *Deploying Django + Python 3 + PostgreSQL to AWS Elastic Beanstalk.* Real Python. Retrieved July 10, 2022, from https://realpython.com/deploying-a-django-app-and-postgresql-to-aws-elastic-beanstalk/

Python, R. (n.d.). *What Can I Do with Python?* Real Python. Retrieved July 9, 2022, from https://realpython.com/what-can-i-do-with-python/

Securing Django Admin. (n.d.). Mastering Django Admin Documentation. https://django-tips.avilpage.com/en/latest/admin_secure.html

Spring Boot Vs Django - Difference between Spring Boot and Django. (2020, December 18). JavaSterling. https://javasterling.com/spring-boot/spring-boot-vs-django/

Sun, S. (2019, September 21). *Deploying a Basic Django App Using Azure App Services.* Major League Hacking. Medium. https://stories.mlh.io/deploying-a-basic-django-app-using-azure-app-services-71ec3b21db08

Templates. (n.d.). Django Documentation | Django. Retrieved July 10, 2022, from https://docs.djangoproject.com/en/4.0/topics/templates/#:~:text

=A%20Django%20template%20is%20a,is%20rendered%20with%20a%20context

URL Dispatcher. (n.d.). Django Documentation | Django. Retrieved July 10, 2022, from https://docs.djangoproject.com/en/4.0/topics/http/urls/

View Decorators. (n.d.). Django Documentation | Django. Retrieved July 10, 2022, from https://docs.djangoproject.com/en/4.0/topics/http/decorators/

What is an IDE? (2019, January 8). Red Hat. https://www.redhat.com/en/topics/middleware/what-is-ide#:~:text=digital%20transformation%20efforts-,Why%20do%20developers%20use%20IDEs%3F,part%20of%20the%20setup%20process

What is AWS? Amazon Cloud (Web) Services Tutorial. (2020, January 5). Guru99. https://www.guru99.com/what-is-aws.html

What is Django? Advantages and Disadvantages of Using Django. (2022, June 7). Hackr.Iohttps://hackr.io/blog/what-is-django-advantages-and-disadvantages-of-using-django

What Is Python Used For? A Beginner's Guide. (n.d.). Coursera. Retrieved July 9, 2022, from https://www.coursera.org/articles/what-is-python-used-for-a-beginners-guide-to-using-python

Widgets. (n.d.). Django Documentation | Django. Retrieved July 10, 2022, from https://docs.djangoproject.com/en/4.0/ref/forms/widgets/

Working with Forms. (n.d.). Django Documentation | Django. Retrieved July 10, 2022, from https://docs.djangoproject.com/en/4.0/topics/forms/#:~:text=Django's%20role%20in%20forms&text=Django%20handles%20three%20distinct%20parts,and%20data%20from%20the%20client

Writing Views. (n.d.). Django Documentation | Django. Retrieved July 10, 2022, from https://docs.djangoproject.com/en/4.0/topics/http/views/

Writing Your First Django App, Part 3. (n.d.). Django Documentation | Django. Retrieved July 9, 2022, from https://docs.djangoproject.com/en/4.0/intro/tutorial03/

Index

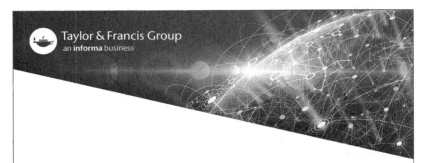